PETER CHURCHILL

PRACTICAL SHOWJUMPING

Photographs by Bob Langrish

HOWELL
BOOK HOUSE

New York

Howell Book House
Macmillan Publishing Company
866 Third Avenue, New York, NY 10022
Collier Macmillan Canada, Inc.

Library of Congress Cataloging-in-Publication Data

Churchill, Peter. 1933–
    Practical showjumping/Peter Churchill – 1st American ed.
      p. cm.
    ISBN 0-87605-887-X
    1. Show jumping. I. Title. II. Title: Practical show jumping.
    SF295.5.C48   1990
    798.2'5–dc20

                                                    89-71744
                                                     CIP

Macmillan books are available at special discounts
for bulk purchases for sales promotions, premiums,
fund-raising, or educational use. For details contact:

Special Sales Director
Macmillan Publishing Company
866 Third Avenue
New York, NY 10022

10 9 8 7 6 5 4 3 2 1

Printed in Great Britain

Contents

CHAPTER 1

Basic Principles and Attitude

WHY A HORSE?

'There is nothing as good for the inside of a man, as the outside of a horse . . .' goes a very famous quotation. Most of the millions of people around the world who are involved with horses would go along with that. Even seasoned professionals who have come up the hard way like Harvey Smith, David Broome, Alwin and Paul Schockemöhle, John Whitaker and Ian Millar, will admit you have got to be 'some sort of horse-freak'.

There is something special about riding a horse whether it be at local or club level, on the Grand Prix circuit, in a dressage arena, over a cross-country course or hacking out and trail-riding through forests or over mountains. What makes it so special? The answer is quite simple. Riding, unlike any other profession, sport or leisure activity, means working with an animal. Not a racket, or a club or a man-made engine or a ball, but a living creature . . . the horse.

A creature that has almost the same spectrum of personality traits and emotions as we do. Like jealousy, lack of confidence, arrogance, determination, fear, honesty and dishonesty. Riding is a relationship between one being and another. An athlete, in the general interpretation, gets himself ready for a race or a field event or a ball game. A riding athlete has to do the same but with the added dimension of working with a living creature. So in showjumping we are working with two athletes.

At this early stage let us clear up the use of him and her in riding for we are, in fact, talking about he or she. So throughout this book I may say him or her, but it is only a general term when I really mean both genders. This is one of the great things about the sport of riding, from showjumping to classical dressage, the exponents, at any level, come from all walks of life. It has never been a sport or pastime restricted by narrow ethnic, cultural or sexual barriers not just for us as members of the human race but also for the horses and

7

ponies involved. There have been many brilliant fillies and mares in horse sports just as much as colts, entires and geldings.

These are the added benefits of our chosen sport or profession. It's not enough to be a good athlete yourself – and we discuss this later in some detail – because riding is all about working with another athlete, the horse. This extra dimension means planning, discipline, both mental and physical, building a relationship of trust and confidence *and* living through the good days and the bad days. This is what makes riding, whether it be showjumping or any other equestrian discipline, very special.

FORMATIVE YEARS

The fundamental principles of horse sports are self-control and the desire to get it right. What more could you ask of a sport? This is what riding has always meant to me. I started as an eleven-year-old child riding for a hard nosed but caring Irish-born dealer. He not only taught me riding but also self-discipline. First the discipline of overcoming fear. Not the fear of getting physically hurt, luckily that never bothered me, but the fear of spoiling a good horse or pony on which we had spent hours, days, weeks, or even months bringing it to its true potential. Potential is a key word in the horse world! Working, even for a short period, in a dealing yard is one of the best forms of training any rider could have as a foundation of a career. Every animal in the yard has to be good at something. As any dealer will tell you – it's no good leaving them in their boxes eating 'money'!

Being good at something may not mean the ability to jump a 5ft (1.5m) fence or move like a ballet dancer. Some horses don't like jumping, and some are born with two left feet. Who says the animal kingdom is any different from ours? But that type of animal can often offer a lovely temperament and an honest character – two assets which are like gold to a riding school, leisure centre or Riding for the Disabled project. So potential can be there in many different ways, if we are prepared to look for it.

The second discipline those formative years taught me was patience, 'Rome was not built in a day' was firmly implanted in my young mind. These characteristics become part of both your working and private life. Riding teaches you discipline and horses can teach us a lot more than we teach them! The dressage rider, for example, spends years building a dialogue between horse and rider.

One speaks to the other through a sensitive system of signals, known as aids. In the jumping horse we are looking for the same thing but in a very different way.

THE JUMPING HORSE AND RIDER

We want the jumping horse to help us when we are wrong . . . and he, the horse, wants us to help him when he is wrong. Let's take a deeper look at that philosophy. Fred Broome Senior, the father of World and European Champion David Broome and Liz Edgar probably the best lady jumping rider in the world, once told me:

> We should only train our horses up to 80 per cent and leave 20 per cent to the horse. Even the best riders get into trouble at least once in a round . . . and when that happens it is that 20 per cent horse which helps them out. It is only the very good, thinking horse that can get out of trouble. That's what makes good jumping horses.

Now Fred Broome is a natural trainer and a very shrewd judge of horses and people and what he is getting at is the very foundation stone of the art of showjumping. The bottom line of the game, in its simplest form, is to be able to ride to the right place at the right time, and in the right frame of mind to jump an unnatural fence cleanly. Showjumping is not about knocking rails down, as equally riding is not about falling off!

If a rider, and most of us do it quite often, misses that simple equation and is not able to ride to the right place at the right time – in other words the rider 'misses his jerk' – then it is only the real jumping horse who will take over, put things right and clear the fence. This is where the *instinct* of the horse and rider take over and it is through this that we encourage the horse to use whatever natural talent and competitive spirit he has. It's what I call the 'grey area' where no coach can go, it belongs to the horse and rider in the arena and only they are capable of producing it at the time it matters.

(pp 10-11)
Ted Edgar (right), his wife Liz (centre) and pupil Janet Hunter. Since retiring from competitive riding Ted Edgar, brother-in-law to David Broome, has become established as one of show jumping's most successful coaches, producing such talent as Nick Skelton, Emma-Jane Mac, Janet Hunter – twice winner of the coveted Queen Elizabeth II Cup – and his own daughter Marie, twice winner of the Junior European Championship gold medal. His wife Liz has won the Queen's Cup a record five times

That is our foundation stone, the element on which the building blocks are going to be placed by careful and programmed training. But those blocks must also be put in the right place at the right time. This is where a coach comes in and he or she must be absolutely part of your life. Your coach must not push you, the student, or your horse too soon but equally both of you should not be held back. Coaching jumping riding is a bit like teaching or helping a baby to walk. Sometimes when the baby falls over it is wrong to move in and keep picking it up. Encouragement, at the right moment, is the key. But it is a delicate balance between mistakes and problems. Many can be used to positive effect but teaching riding, in any form, must never be allowed to develop into a negative situation. No matter what happens something positive must be found at each stage.

Attitude and Aptitude

The gifted American coach, George Morris, has always said: 'Give me attitude before aptitude'. What does George mean by that?

Attitude is being disciplined; being a good learner; putting your confidence in your coach; listening to your horse; caring how your horse goes and how he approaches showjumping; attitude is that often disliked word . . . dedication.

Aptitude, on the other hand, is talent. But talent alone, no matter how gifted, is not enough. Talent can only produce results if it is controlled and guided along the right path with each step carefully thought out. And George Morris is right! Talent comes in and out of showjumping with the passing of every year. But a talented rider without the right attitude seems to disappear as quickly as he arrived if he cannot take or get the right coaching. When attitude and aptitude are handled correctly it can take a rider to the very top and if the attitude is constant that rider will stay at the top.

Jumping riding can be taught in a precise manner and if that system is followed and guided with intelligence then the results can be predictable. 'If there is a secret to this game, it's getting the right instructor at the beginning of your career,' Alwin Schockemöhle, Olympic Gold medallist at the 1976 Montreal Olympic Games once told me and he added: 'As for the horse, it's the level of the handling he has experienced *before* he starts his jumping career that counts.'

Alwin raises two very important points. Firstly, getting the right coach does not necessarily mean the most celebrated one but the right one for you. A coach you feel confident with. A coach who is interested in you and your horse. A coach you feel has the professional ability and experience to bring you through each phase of your riding at just the right time. The last thing you need is an egotist who spends your time showing you what he can do! But, perhaps, the golden rule of all golden rules, is once you have found the right coach for you, don't go switching around from one trainer to another every few months or weeks. Consistency will always get results and continuity ensures progress. Don't just go to a coach when you have a problem. You will need regular help to make real progress.

The second point Alwin was making is that the standard of a horse's training on the flat will determine not only how good a showjumper he is going to be, but also how consistent a performer he will be in the show ring.

Be wary of a coach who spends most of the early sessions telling the student: 'You have been using the wrong system!' We hear so much on this subject and it is, on the whole, totally uninformed and at least misguided. Terms like the German system, the American system or the French or Italian and so on, are really the same product wrapped differently and presented according to the type of horse being used. To claim that the German horse is more disciplined than, say, the American horse, is just a home-spun fantasy in the modern world of showjumping. The Americans, the English and the French 'drill' their jumpers just as much as any German rider does. They *all* aim to produce willing and obedient jumping horses in the show ring.

Style and Technique

Where there is a difference it lies in style not system. All jumping riders and trainers now, particularly at international level, produce

(pp 14-15)
Harvey Smith, discussing a course with the genial American coach, Bertalan de Nemethy. The American showjumping team was all-conquering under the guidance of de Nemethy, an ex-Hungarian Cavalry officer who believes very strongly that to be consistenly successful all competitive riding must be based on the classical principles of equitation
(inset) Harvey Smith, possibly the most successful showjumping rider in the history of the sport. Harvey has never had a riding lesson in his life, but he is a natural horseman with a dedicated eye for detail. 'Watch the best, study them and learn' is Harvey's philosophy

their horses and riders along the same principles of equitation, lightness, balance, activity, rhythm and willingness. The style that evolves in any country is governed by local needs. For example, the American jumping horse comes up through equitation classes, green and field hunter classes and amateur/owner classes. In North America, for example, the young horse and rider start out by being judged on jumping technique over a 'natural' course set at even strides. Points are gained for style of both horse and rider.

In West Germany the youngsters start off their competitive careers in dressage and dressage with jumping. In Britain and Ireland, the development of the sport is firmly based on pony jumping with young riders coming in at a very early age to straight competitive jumping. No other country in the world has what one might call a 'full-time' national pony circuit.

Why theorise about sport? Our ability in a sport tends to progress from the basic level the more we get involved, and the more we get involved the better we want to do it. Showjumping is a good example of this for most competitors start out, not too seriously, at Pony Club/Riding Club level, or unaffiliated shows, but before very long they are setting their sights on something higher.

Let us, then, take as the basic philosophy of this book the idea that the better we play a game, the more exciting and satisfying the results will be. But before we can build on this foundation, we must decide what type of competitor we are going to be, for, there is more than one way to approach showjumping as a competitive game.

Wherever one goes in the world equitation comes down to two basic schools of thought. These can be divided into proponents of the 'physical rider' and the 'technical rider'.

The physical rider relies on his natural dominance of the horse as a vehicle to achieve the rider's aims such as winning a competition with complete disregard for style, technique or manner in which it is achieved. They 'over-ride' their horses, never letting the animal think for himself. But these riders usually have a very sharp competitive spirit, a talent for split-second timing and the gymnastic ability to pivot on their knees to give their horses freedom in the air. But on the flat they keep complete physical control of their horses. These riders, many of them gifted in their own way, are what international team coaches call 'flair-riders'.

The physical school follows a simple system – given the strength and gymnastic balance it is not all that difficult to influence the

16

mind and body of a domesticated animal. But the system produces its own drawbacks. The results, although sometimes brilliant, tend to be inconsistent and the wear and tear on the horse is considerable. This domination is more apparent, unfortunately, in junior pony jumping than anywhere else. Most trainers are too tall or too heavy to school ponies under saddle, so artificial methods, such as complicated bits or short martingales, have to be used to help the young rider who lacks experience and strength. The shame is that this has a knock-on effect on that young rider's technique and attitude in later life.

The technical rider, on the other hand, follows a graduated schooling programme which has as its base the aim of educating both horse and rider to work together as a team with the minimum and simplest forms of intervention by the rider. Where the physical school tends to over-ride, the technical rider tends to under- ride in order to encourage the horse to use his natural ability as an athlete and his flair and power.

What may seem to be a drawback to some is that the technical school, as we are defining it, takes a lot more time and hard work on the part of the rider to produce a young horse. The basic schooling on the flat must be thorough and the early work over poles on the ground and small fences must be meticulously carried out. Also attention to detail has to be given to other areas such as the feeding programme and the general well-being of the horse. Everything must come together to produce a horse and rider who are both mentally calm and confident while also being fit, alert and very supple.

The benefits of the system are consistent results and performance once horse and rider have gained some show experience as well as very little wear and tear on the horse either physically or mentally. Riding a horse, be it for pleasure or in competition, should not be a battle. Horses can enjoy competing and for a rider there is nothing better than sitting on a horse which has been correctly schooled and handled. All the trophies in the world cannot replace that marvellous feeling of satisfaction when you come out of the arena knowing your horse has jumped a copy-book round.

Theory is one thing, actually putting it into practice is another. All jumping riders should certainly strive to use correct and polished techniques but following a pattern or doctrine is not enough in itself, the rider *must want to jump and win*. The same can be said of the horse, trained and schooled to physical and mental peak but that will not be enough unless the horse likes jumping and is full of courage. Those two factors are the '20 per cent' Fred Broome was talking about, that 'grey area', which belongs to the rider. Only in the best possible world will a novice horse or rider move through a graduated training and schooling programme without placing a foot wrong. There are compensations for there can be fewer more satisfying sights than seeing an educated, physically fit horse jumping fences willingly and gracefully. Showjumping is one of the clearest expressions of the sport of riding and the success of completing a course of show fences, laid out and designed by someone else, with style, technique and fluency is just as good a proof of horsemanship as a mantelshelf covered with cups, medals and ribbons. If the initial aims of the preliminary training programme are achieved – a calm, educated horse with a supple, well-balanced rider – then the red ribbons will not be all that far away.

NATURAL AND TRAINED BEHAVIOUR

Why all this emphasis on graduated schooling and programmed training schedules? The answer to that is the partnership which must be achieved between horse and rider. The horse is not one of nature's jumping animals, as the cat and dog families are. He has no soft paws, his body is rigid compared to that of the dog or cat. When left to themselves the majority of horses will show no inclination and very little aptitude for leaping over any object that may cross their path or restrict their freedom. Even when fleeing from danger or in panic, most horses will crash through whatever gets in their way.

Many experiments have been carried out to test and explain this difference between 'natural' and 'trained' behaviour. A particularly interesting one was set up in the United States some years ago. A group of horses, old, young, trained and untrained, were put in a post-and-rail paddock with poor pasture next to another paddock with lush good pasture. It was found that something like 90 to 95 per cent of the group remained in the poor paddock or tried to stick their heads through the railings to get at the good pasture. Some injured themselves, others broke the rails but the few that did jump over to the greener grass were *all* trained horses.

Therefore we will be working from the basis that the horse is not a 'natural' jumping animal, in the true meaning of the word, but he can develop into a powerful and efficient athlete. The rider's job is both a physical and mental one; his movements and actions are at all times directly relevant to the athletic ability and natural grace of the horse. Showjumping is a gymnastic exercise and the horse does need to be educated to it. That education is achieved by getting the horse's body fit and supple and his mind relaxed and confident. We must keep in mind that showjumping is asking the unnatural in so much as the horse goes into a ring on his own (away from the other horses) and must clear the fences.

The student rider has to undergo a similar education in many ways. He has to be fit and supple, too, with a relaxed and confident mental attitude and a riding standard that in no way hinders or un-balances the horse.

DRESS

Finally before we move on to discuss all these aims we have out-lined let's take a look at dress. A strange subject to bring up in a book on improving your showjumping, you might think. But is it? A good craftsman never blames his tools but equally a real craftsman always makes sure he has the best tools he can find. The same principles apply with the correct dress for training. A runner has his tracksuit, 'trainers' etc, so too must a rider.

There are three main rules to follow: 1 Be smart; 2 Be comfort-able; and 3 Be safe! Sloppy dress means sloppy thinking. A lot of time and trouble is put into turning out the horse each day – or certainly should be – so don't insult that by neglecting your own turn-out.

There are two effective styles of dress for training. A pair of suede or leather chaps over jeans or lightweight trousers and breeches and boots. If you wear breeches then, of course, you will have boots but with chaps a pair of jodphur boots or western boots are best . . . and safest! No 'trainers', please!

On your head, a hard velvet hunting style cap, properly fitted, and with a chin harness or jockey skull crash helmet with a silk, velvet or woollen cover over it.

Warm gloves are essential in winter but lightweight gloves are, I think, a great help to comfort in the summer. In the daily routine of training the reins can get sweaty and that is certainly not comfortable.

Finally, a short stick or a long schooling whip for some flat-work and a pair of blunt spurs. The stick, whether it is short or

long, and the spurs are not for punishing the horse. They are purely and simply there to back up the rider's legs and seat aids. We are, after all, trying to achieve a positive dialogue with the jumping horse. We are also going to need quick answers from the horse in the show ring. None of these will be achieved by the rider kicking and thumping with heels and legs like the popular Thelwell Pony Club cartoon character! There is more than enough for the rider to be doing while jumping without the added complication of swinging his legs around all over the place. The horse, too, must find all that flapping around an aggravating handicap.

Dressed for training: jodphur boots, a pair of suede or leather chaps and a hard hat with chinstrap

CHAPTER 2

The Right Horse

TEMPERAMENT

Before we can discuss the ideal make and shape of a jumping horse, we have first of all to study the mechanics of the animal's body when jumping a show fence. For the purpose of showjumping we are looking for certain vital points in the horse's physical make-up that may not be so important, or even needed, in the horse which is being used for showing, dressage or cross-country jumping.

The first factor we have to allow for is that unlike other forms of riding where jumping is involved, like hunting, point-to-pointing, steeplechasing, eventing and team cross-country riding, show-jumping has to be performed 'cold'. This means that the horse does not have the incentives of herd instinct unlike the horse racing over fences with a group of other runners or the advantage of speed to make height or length over an obstacle as in cross-country riding. So the showjumping horse must be capable of performing on his own, under varying conditions, over all kinds of different fences and at a variety of paces according to different classes and conditions from a preliminary round to a jump-off against the clock.

Physical make-up is obviously important as this helps good balance, but temperament and aptitude for intensive and athletic training is essential for the showjumping horse. This is the 'heart', the personality and character of the horse and it has to be considered just as much as the perfect lines of the body. In showjumping we need a 'thinking' horse. A horse with a beautiful body and no brains will still be a novice jumper when he is twenty years old!

Physique

Muscular power and free-flowing movement are the essence of the jumping horse. The activity and the strength of the hindquarters and the hind legs are the source of the lift that takes the horse into the air. Often mistakenly one hears the term 'spring' used. Horses cannot spring although there has been the odd little one that has given a very good impression of it, but they are very rare indeed.

An easy striding action is the basis of the jumping horse's balance and rhythm. Sound limbs are essential for support in take-off and for accepting the shock of landing. The horse's hooves have to act as shock absorbers therefore the strain on the limbs, particularly the lower limbs, is considerable. Good round feet are needed with plenty of interior space for protection as the weight of the horse comes to the ground on landing. The head and neck form the balancing pole and the back is both a support and an extension of this balance.

The trained jumper should jump out of his stride, which means he should not be *forced* back onto his hindquarters in order to go into the air and over the fence. Equally a situation should not arise where the horse is so over-restricted that he is left with no option but to dance in front of the fence in order to stoke up the power to take his fence.

THE JUMPING OUTLINE

On the approach to a fence the horse lowers his head and stretches his neck. What he is doing is looking for the ground-line or baseline of the fence so that he can measure the height. In doing so he can regulate his stride, balance himself and prepare his hocks (hind legs) for the take-off. The horse gets his elevation from the power of his hocks.

On arriving at the point of take-off, the horse shortens his neck and brings his hocks well under his body. It is the strength of his hocks and the evenness of his stride which pushes the forehand up and into the air. This strength and ability to balance the stride differs, of course, from horse to horse depending on his make and shape. This is the difference between the horse's jumping technique and that of 'natural' jumping animals. The horse does not lift his forehand, he supports it with his hocks and pushes it upwards with his hind legs.

As the horse begins to go into the air he stretches his head and neck further and downwards, once again for balance, and makes his trajectory upwards and forwards. The hind legs and hocks give the final push to leave the ground. Once in the air, the period of suspension above the obstacle, the horse has his head and neck extended to the maximum. The head and neck now, once more for balance, are taking a more acute downward attitude for the back to form a bridge over the fence. The hind legs start to follow the line of the 'bridge' while the forelegs begin to fold up. This is what the professional trainers call a horse that 'snaps up' in front or 'folds up'.

To examine the jumping outline more closely let's simplify the whole operation by going back to basics. The object of showjumping, as against any other horse sport, is to get the animal to clear a fence without knocking a rail off. So as the horse measures his fence from the bottom upwards the action of his front legs is an indication of how accurate he has been in that calculation because it is his front legs that will meet the rail first. An animal which does this accurately can be termed a careful jumping horse.

Malcolm Pyrah, one of the best horsemen on the international circuit, explains:

> . . . When the horse folds up in front, the forelegs, either at the knee or at the pastern, must be together. If the horse leaves one foreleg dangling, then that's the one which will have a rail down. It is the higher foreleg that the horse snaps up which is the one he has measured the fence by. I would rather see them leave a hind leg trailing than a foreleg. You have more chance of getting away with that!

There is a lot of commonsense in what Malcolm says, for after all, there is no point in going into the ring if you know your horse is going to kick out rails just to get to the finishing line.

The next stage will be the horse preparing himself for landing. The first development here will be the unfolding of the front legs as they reach for the ground and the hind legs will be thrown up behind the horse to complete the bridge of his back over the arc of the fence. So the horse will be reaching forward with his front legs to take the shock of landing, extending his hind legs to counterbalance the forward movement. A horse that is capable of jumping with this technique is known, through the classical theory, as having a bascule over a fence. And what does bascule amount to? Balance is the secret of the horse with a 'natural' aptitude for jumping show fences. As the horse prepares to land he also raises his head and shortens his neck because the forelegs and the shoulders must now take the strain of landing as the hindquarters and the hocks did at the point of take-off.

As the front legs land and touch the ground so the hind legs begin to follow through to complete the landing. They start to come under the horse ready to push his body forward into the recovery stride after landing. At the same time the head and neck is lowered and extended ready for the entire sequence to begin again for the next obstacle.

We will be discussing, later in this book, how the rider works in unison, or takes advantage, of this sequence. But at this early stage let's just take a closer look at the working parts we would like to see in our ideal jumping horse . . .

CONFORMATION

The Feet
These should be round and large enough to support the horse's bodyweight. Small feet, for example, on a large horse or big feet on a light horse, will make him difficult to train. The sole of the foot should be slightly but definitely concave. This will give the horse a better foothold. The frog should be well defined and rubber-like to touch.

Care of the feet is of paramount importance in producing competition horses. They must have regular attention from the farrier. They must be kept clean and the horse's bedding material should be fresh and dry at all times. 'No foot, no horse' may be a hackneyed old phrase but it says it all.

The Pasterns
These should be long, well sloped and strong-looking. Too straight a pastern, or too short a one, will hinder the stride of the horse in the extended and shortened gaits. We will later see that the ability to change 'gear' from one length of stride to another is absolutely vital to the jumping horse.

The Cannon and Tendons
These should be short and strong as they take most of the strain in jumping. If the cannon and tendon are too long, or too finely boned, they will not stand up to intensive training, let alone the pounding they will have to take in the competition arena.

The Knees and Hocks
The knee-joints and the hock-joints should be large, bony and flat. These form the vital hinges in the horse's jumping technique, so the larger and flatter they are the more flexible and efficient they will be.

The Forearm and Shoulder

The forearm should be set well into the chest and the shoulders with a pronounced muscular shape, rather like the developed biceps of a human athlete. The shoulders should be flat rather than fleshy, sloping well back to the wither to give the maximum pendulum action, making the lengthening and shortening of strides graceful and easy.

Chest and Girth

The chest should be deep when looked at from the front and from the side. A broad-based, deep, chest will allow plenty of heart room. The heart pumps blood around the body at varying rates. During periods of rest the rate is slower than when approaching a show fence or, indeed, when jumping a treble combination, or in a jump-off against the clock. At times of maximum effort the heart rate is at its fastest. The heart expands and contracts to pump blood around the body. A large chest cavity facilitates expansion with the least effort. One large expansion, followed by a maximum contraction, puts less strain on the heart's function than several short expansions followed by quick short contractions.

A deep line through the girth is not enough for the performance horse. Depth alone will not give heart space, it must be accompanied by width. The width of the chest, though, should not be so exaggerated as to appear heavy or clumsy, as this is likely to be reflected in the horse's jumping technique. Also the depth and width of the chest must be in proportion to the girth. The lungs, like the heart, are at their simplest a pumping apparatus for the processing of oxygen. Again, in a narrow horse the lungs will be restricted. So the barrel of the body and the rib-cage should be well rounded, tapering into the loin and hip areas.

The Back

A short back is better than a long back in the jumping horse and one good way of judging the back is to imagine the horse under saddle. The ideal back should be short enough for the rider and saddle to fit comfortably into the middle of the horse with very little left over between the back of the saddle and the horse's hip-joint. A horse which is too long in the back will not be easy to train or to get really fit and supple as true balance will be very difficult to achieve. The rib-cage should be well sprung and come right up to the hip-joint. It should also be just a little flat in shape. A rib-cage which is too

26

round will make it difficult for the rider to give accurate and positive leg aids.

The wither should be well defined so that the saddle settles securely and comfortably in the correct area of the back.

The Tail

This is often overlooked in analyses of conformation. The tail is an extension of the spine and back so its position and the way the horse carries it is, I think, quite a vital clue as to how the horse will use his back when jumping. Although the horse cannot bend his spine in the true sense (again not like the dog and the cat), we do require him to 'bend' or 'tip' over the top of a show fence.

Former senior international, Freddie Welch, now a top coach himself, put it more graphically: 'I like to see a jumper pour over his fence, like milk coming out of a jug.'

I like to see a tail set high and carried with pride. A horse that flags his tail tends to be supple in his back muscles, whereas a horse that tucks his tail tends to be stiff in his back.

The Neck and Head

The neck should be long, taper into the head and not be set too low into the shoulders and breast area. A good neck and front is what is known as 'plenty of rein'. Such a horse will be easier to bridle and school, having natural balance from his length of rein, whereas a horse that is short or thick of neck will have balance problems when ridden and the rider will have problems in jumping schooling.

If a horse is too light in the neck he will tend to overbend, through lack of strength in that area, to his bridle. The neck is the horse's balancing pole, so its length and depth should be relative to the length and depth of the horse's body.

Bold large ears are said to denote a generous nature and nine times out of ten that old yardstick is very accurate.

A nice head should be broad at the top, tapering to the nose, with well-rounded, wide nostrils. The horse's eyes should be set low in the head, large in shape and wide apart. I like to see a horse looking out at the world rather than one who lets the world look at him.

So we have worked our way through our perfect jumping horse. But just how important is conformation? The answer is simple – vital! If a horse is correctly made with each part in proportion to the other, training will be easier and will be attained without undue strain on the horse's framework. In other words he will be a better ride and be less prone to injury. But the student has to be careful not to get too indoctrinated by hard-and-fast rules. There is a science to assessing a horse as an athlete. To be able to spot that 'magic ingredient' of a truly good horse can take years of practice. Experience and observation are the best indicators when it comes to the complex, delicate and sometimes ambiguous subject of assessing horses and their potential.

ADAPTATION

The private owner, such as a senior Pony Club or Riding Club member, who already has a horse which may not fit the ideal picture of the traditional lines of conformation should not despair. There is a good solid old saying in the horse world: 'To his good points be forever kind and to his bad faults be forever blind.' There is a lot of truth in that old saying. One of the best international jumpers I ever had was certainly no oil painting. His back was far too long, he had a very pronounced roman nose, his legs were too long and so on but on the plus side he had tremendous power in his hind legs, he was very bold – sometimes too much for his own good – and he was a brilliant mover with a natural cadence and bounce to his stride. This last point is one that is often underrated in the continual analysis we hear so often on discussions of the make and shape of a showjumper. It's very nice to have the perfectly made horse, but without the right kind of action even the best made horses are not going to make showjumpers.

Obviously make and shape are important factors as for any athlete but for showjumping we are not looking for a show horse with an extravagant movement. The long-striding horse which points his front toe with elegance and glides over the ground may impress a show judge but whether he will make a showjumper is another question altogether. In the showjumper it is vital that the horse's action must be such that he can shorten and lengthen his stride naturally. To be able to do that the jumping horse has a rounder action with more bend of his knee and hocks than one would see in the ideal show horse. The old saying: 'springs in his heels' happens to be true and the jumping horse, whether he be a cross-country horse, a steeplechaser or a showjumper must have a bounce in his stride. It's from his stride that he gets his spring, so often confused with a natural jump.

IDEAL TYPES

For many experts the great showjumping horse is a freak. I have even heard the same comfortable label given to great steeplechasers like Arkle. In Great Britain, where there is no controlled breeding programme for sport horses, other than Thoroughbreds, this freak label is most probably accurate. We only have to look at some of the jumping stars of the past like the pony-sized Stroller.

Ralph Coakes's brilliant little Stroller was first registered with the British Show Jumping Association as a pony. But his daughter, Marion, now married to former Royal steeplechase jockey, David Mould, decided to take him on when she moved up to competing in the senior division. The 14.2hh Irish-bred gelding captured the hearts of the nation when taking Marion to success in the Hickstead Derby, the Ladies World Championship, the Queen Elizabeth II Cup at the Royal International Horse Show, the British Grand Prix (the John Player Trophy), the Leading Show Jumper of the Year title, a second John Player Trophy, Queen's Cup and National Championship and an individual silver medal at the 1968 Mexico Olympic Games. What is remarkable about Stroller's record is that he was beating horses at world-class level which were some 6–8in (15–20cm) taller than him.

At the other end of the spectrum was another so-called freak, Fred Hartill's Pennwood Forge Mill. Forgie was big and long in all the ways that Stroller was not! Yet under Paddy McMahon the Irish-bred gelding won or was placed in 600 National and International competitions, including a European championship, the King George V Gold Cup, the Ronson Trophy, two Horse and Hound Cups, three Texaco Championships and won or was placed in fifty-one Area International Trials. As Fred Hartill has always said: 'Conformation is one thing, but always look to what is in the heart of a horse because in the end that's the winning factor'. Many racehorse trainers would agree with that statement.

In modern showjumping would the Strollers and Forge Mills of the past be the stars of today? There is no way we can make accurate comparisons because we are not relating like to like. Today in showjumping at national and international level we are increasingly seeing the custom-bred horse, through European breeding programmes, dominate the sport. Even in Great Britain, the top horse of the late eighties, Mr and Mrs Tom Bradley's Next Milton, is a custom-bred sports horse and certainly no freak. The fabulous grey was sired by the Dutch stallion Marius, a world-class jumping horse under their late daughter Caroline, and out of a mare who bred a Foxhunter champion. His rider John Whitaker is the first to admit that this prolific winner of Grands Prix all over the world is a born and bred showjumper.

The West Germans, the French, the Belgians, the Scandinavians and the Dutch have proved that the breeding of a showjumping horse is not a question of accident. Each has used many generations of their own native breeds such as carriage horses and farm horses mixed with Thoroughbred blood to produce a horse with the temperament to cope with intensive training and demanding competition in the show arena, the cross-country course and the dressage arena. Horses like Paul Schockemöhle's Hanoverian-bred Deister, which carried him to three consecutive European Championship titles and won over DM1m in his career. Deister, like so many European Warmbloods, a term given to clean-bred horses which come from native lines as against the Thoroughbred, was bred for the job. Sired by Diskant, one of West Germany's top jumping stallions, Deister was sold out of a Hanoverian Horse Society Elite Auction Sale as a potential young show jumper. There are many other examples like Austrian rider Hugo Simon's Gladstone, by Gotz and bred down the famous Hanoverian G line created by the jumping stallion Gotthard; the Hanoverian Mr T, which carried Canadian Gail Greenough to a World Championship title; the Trakehner stallion Abdullah, winner of the Winter World Cup finals, an Olympic silver medal and a World Championship silver medallist for American rider Conrad Homfeld; the Dutch-bred Apollo, ridden to so many international successes by our own Nick Skelton and the French Olympic Champion Jappeloup de Luze ridden by Pierre Durand.

Its not just at world-class level where we are seeing these Warmblood or custom-bred horses coming through in showjumping. In North America they have taken over from the once popular Thoroughbred ex-racehorse. This has happened over a period of years by design. The European breeders and their breed societies, in some cases through indirect government help from state betting monopolies, run stallion and mare performance and grading systems with close monitoring of youngstock: the end-product is a clean-bred non-Thoroughbred horse which can be placed in two categories as potential jumping horses or potential dressage horses. There is no claim that every single one of them is going to be an Olympic star but at least, the buyer knows that he can look at a bunch of young horses knowing that they have been bred with a suitable temperament, make and shape, and ability for equestrian sport at some level.

BUYING A YOUNG HORSE

Buying a young jumping horse is not the high-risk adventure it used to be when the only avenue open to the first-time buyer was the classified advertisements in the equestrian press. The buyer can now bring the hit or miss factor down to less of a game of chance. But many private owners still start by looking at the price of a horse . . . saying: 'Ah yes, now this one I can afford,' and work back from there. True enough, they will get the horse at the price they want to pay but they may not get the horse to suit them and more often than not they will finish up buying someone else's problems!

What is the best way for a private buyer to go shopping for a young jumping horse? Or for a new horse to replace an old one? The first step is tied up with George Morris's point – attitude – you want to be quite clear in your mind that you are going to go slowly and that you want to see and try as many horses as you can. Now if you do this by answering classified advertisements you could find yourself spending almost as much money and time running around from one end of the country to the other on abortive journeys as you would spend keeping your horse for six months. It is better by far to go to an established professional dealer where you can go and see – and try – several horses in one morning.

Without contacts in the horse business how do you find a professional dealer? Well, there are two ways of approaching this. Firstly, if you are or have been a member of your local Pony Club then you can turn to your District Commissioner for advice. He or she will know the dealers in your area. Secondly the Equestrian Trade Association publishes a directory every year and one section includes a list of professional dealers who are members of that trade organisation (see Useful Addresses). Have a look down the list and sort out your own short-list of the dealers in your area. Then ring them up, tell them what you are looking for and make an appointment to see them.

Many books advise that you take an 'expert' with you when you go buying and I think there was a certain soundness in that in the days when people bought through private sellers. But if you go to a professional dealer it would be better not to turn up with your expert friend. Nine times out of ten you will find that your 'expert' will spend most of his or her time trying to impress the dealer with knowledge rather than thinking about your needs. That can lead to a very frustrating morning both for you and the dealer.

Horse dealers are in the business of selling horses. It is in their interest to sell you, if they can, a horse suitable for you and your needs for two very logical reasons: firstly they want you to come back again for your next horse or even another one, and secondly, even in this day and age horse dealers still believe that the best form of advertising is word of mouth.

But the avenues open to horse-buyers, and not just first-time ones, are far greater than just a trip to a local dealer. All of the Warmblood breeders' associations in Europe run their own auction sales of selected young horses. One of the main advantages of buying in this way is that the horses have been carefully selected and graded into two groups, jumping horses and dressage horses. Many of the breed societies have created another group under the heading, hunters. These are young horses which have shown an aptitude for jumping with a more showy movement on the flat.

The Hanoverian Horse Breeders Society, based in Verden, West Germany, is a good example of how this works. Each year the society selects, through their registered breeders, a group of some one hundred young horses which are then produced by the society's riders and trainers for one of its annual auction sales. When sale time comes they are graded into jumping, dressage and hunter groups. They are all veterinary inspected and their full breeding, going back several generations, is checked and recorded.

Mr and Mrs Tom Bradley's Next Milton with John Whitaker in the saddle. Milton is the perfect model of the ideal we look for in the jumping horse – a natural athlete with a calm and obedient temperament. Milton was bred for the sport, being sired by the Dutch stallion Marius which carried the late Caroline Bradley to so many international successes. His dam came from a well-known jumping line, which included a Foxhunter Champion

Our willing model throughout this book – Rollo, with his owner Maureen Collins. Rollo has all the right qualities in the right places: an intelligent head, deep, strong body, short back and good limbs

Janet Hunter's Irish-bred Everest Lisnamarrow
shows the athleticism and power we look for in the
showjumping horse. Before Janet joined the Ted
Edgar team, she and her father produced
Lisnamarrow from an untrained novice to grade A
level

The Irish team horse, Glendalough, ridden by
Cdt Gerry Mullins, gives us a good illustration of
the meaning of 'having rein'. His neck is bringing
the rest of his body into balance as he reaches the
highest point of his jump, and Gerry has given
him the freedom to use that balancing pole. Again
we see that look of intelligence about the horse's
head

35

Malcolm Pyrah on Towerlands Anglezarke, with a simple D-ringed snaffle.
and a running martingale fitted to give the horse freedom in the air, but short
enough to help Malcolm control Anglezarke on the flat

The cross-over or flash noseband has become the most popular in showjumping
of the many varieties of the drop-noseband. West Germany's Franke Sloothaak
gives us the perfect example of how any drop-noseband should be fitted. It is
positioned to give the rider the maximum help by encouraging the horse to 'give'
to the bridle, and it is placed well away from the horse's nostrils. Notice also that
Sloothaak has kept his equipment simple . . . and look at the freedom he gives
his horse over a fence

We turn again to Malcolm Pyrah and Towerlands Anglezarke for an excellent illustration of a jumping horse really using his 'engine', the hindquarters. The complete picture is one of power, rhythm, balance and action – this horse really is an 'uphill' ride

The late Caroline Bradley and the Dutch stallion Marius, sire of Milton whom Caroline produced as a young horse. You will see that in this competition Caroline has Marius in a hackamore or bitless bridle. These are often used in showjumping when a horse has had a mouth injury or other problem, is recovering from recent dental treatment such as rasping to take off any rough edges which may have developed on the teeth, or sometimes, quite simply, to give the horse a change. The bitless bridle looks simple, but in inexperienced hands it can, in fact, be very severe. So do not be tempted to fit a bitless bridle before seeking expert advice on the techniques for using it

Prior to the sales buyers can inspect the horses and, if they wish to, try out the ones that they are interested in. All the horses in the sales are put through their paces, on the flat, over fences and jumping loose and potential buyers can see and study each horse individually. As each horse enters the sales ring his full breeding is given and an assessment of his temperament and ability is made.

These sales attract buyers from all over the world who are looking for potential international horses for dressage and jumping and many 'stars' have emerged such as Paul Schockemöhle's Hanoverian-bred Deister and Dr Reiner Klimke's Ahlerich, winner of the individual dressage gold medal at the 1984 Olympic Games. Horses of that potential, obviously, fetch strong prices and very competitive bidding but don't be put off. As in Thoroughbred sales, there are plenty of good young horses ideally suited to the amateur competition rider.

If you buy a young horse which has been broken, is riding away and jumping small coloured fences through a local dealer you will pay from £1,500 to £2,500. For a young horse which already has a track record in the ring at novice competition level then your price range is going to be from £3,000 to £5,000. If you buy through one of the European breed societies auction sales then the price range is going to be from £2,000 to £4,000 and it might cost you something like £400 to ship the horse home.

Keeping a competition horse at home, quite apart from any capital expenditure, costs about £2,000 per year. To keep that same horse in a professional yard, a livery or training establishment, will cost the owner anything from £4,000 per year upwards. I know of several golf, sailing and motor-rally enthusiasts who spend as much as that or more per annum on their chosen sport. But in equestrian sport you can't lock the horse up in the garage for a week when you don't need him! Owning a horse or pony is a full-time commitment and responsibility. He has to be looked after seven days a week and fifty-two weeks of the year. In most showjumping families that means holidays are out for a start! But that is the main attraction for horse-sport enthusiasts . . . working with and competing with a living creature.

David Broome and his Olympic horse, Queensway Countryman. David never hesitates to express the importance of the foundation to his long and successful career established by his father, Fred senior – and it shows! His horse is supple, using his body well and has that look of real concentration on his job

CHAPTER 3

Training Facilities and Equipment

No matter what purpose the horse is going to be used for, whether as a jumper, show horse or just for pleasure, some form of dressage training must be given so that the horse will carry himself and his rider in a balanced and comfortable manner.

Dressage means different things to different people. To some it is a form of competition, to others almost a circus act and to a third group a closed book but to the future jumping horse a form of basic dressage training is essential. First we have to be clear in our own minds what we mean by basic dressage in jumping training.

In the general sense there are two forms of dressage. One as a basis of training which is essential to the physical and mental performance of the sporting horse, and the other is dressage as a competitive sport. Dressage means – purely and simply – obedience and suppleness. The combination of mental attitude and physical training is contained in that one word. But in jumping training we can add a deeper meaning to the term; that of education relating both to the horse and the rider.

EASY DEVELOPMENT

The wild horse undergoes many physical changes in the early years of his life. He starts out as a timid, inquisitive foal running with his mother and the herd. His emotional security comes from being a member of the group. But as he grows older he learns to face life within the herd on his own four feet as he develops into a gangling and leggy young horse. His life now begins to follow the seasons in search of mineral- and vitamin-rich food, sometimes galloping, sometimes making quick changes of direction and crossing mountains and plains. Every day life becomes more serious and his body develops all the time. It becomes more muscular, more powerful, and his legs become stronger. His mental reflexes get sharper. So from the little foal that wobbled around the feet of his mother some four years earlier has emerged an adult horse – strong, quick and confident of himself and his surroundings.

The domesticated horse, on the other hand, cannot develop along the same lines as his wild brother. Yet, as in the dog and other domesticated animals, the herd instinct and curiosity is substituted by man and his horse management. These become the substitutes for nature. Dressage, in its broadest sense takes over the physical and mental development of the horse and man becomes his herd. So from this basis dressage, the basic training on the flat of the jumping horse, comes in as a substitute for nature, guiding the horse to physical and mental maturity.

The aim of dressage, in the sense we mean it, is to develop the mind and body through a medium of gymnastic exercises to improve the horse's use of his mind, increase his muscle development and to carefully programme the transition from the natural to the man-made. But the exercises carried out to improve a horse's obedience are directly orientated to the education of his mind rather than the domination of the rider over the horse.

BASIC TRAINING

What determines whether or not the domesticated horse is a good ride? (We will discuss later what the rider's responsibilities are!) At this stage let's keep in our minds that we should ride in such a way that the horse does not find it uncomfortable or unpleasant. True enough, he does not have much choice but he will soon learn that the better he goes the easier his job will be. Good horses make good riders: good riders make bad horses better and bad riders make good horses worse!

What makes a good ride?

- The horse should go forward freely with a balanced rhythm
- The horse must have a steady headcarriage
- The horse should be smooth in all gaits and in jumping
- The horse should move 'straight'
- The horse must be supple and confident of his physical ability
- The horse must *willingly* obey his rider's aids

All this cannot be achieved overnight; it is going to take hard concentrated work by both horse and rider. There are absolutely no short-cuts. They will only result in some incurable side-effects.

The horse should go forward freely and with rhythm. Rollo and Addie are giving us a nice illustration of that principle — plenty of activity in the hindquarters, the horse is giving his mouth and the rider is on a light contact

Training facilities at home. It is not vital to have an all-weather arena or an expensive indoor school for working at home. An area of 'old' grass, well sheltered and drained, will be more than adequate, providing you rotate which part of it you work in each day or week, depending on weather conditions

The so-called dressage training has to be carefully programmed. Horse and rider have to be completely proficient at any one stage before going onto the next.

TRAINING AREA

Very little is required in specialised equipment. All that is needed is a flat, well-sheltered area measuring some 150 x 60ft (45.7 x 18.3m). It should be well drained and have a good covering of grass. Nothing has a more negative effect on a horse's action than uneven or hard going. But it is not always as easy as it sounds for if the surface is grass it will only be available in certain types of weather conditions. If it gets too wet, no matter how well drained it might be, the surface will become poached and uneven, and if it gets too dry the surface will get hard and often dusty.

The answer to all these disadvantages is an all-weather schooling arena. There are several ways you can go about achieving this . . .

- Have an all-weather surface of wood-bark or chippings laid down by a specialist firm
- Make your own with the help of a local landscape gardener or builder

Which of these methods you follow will, of course, depend on how much you want to spend. I have built and designed several with the help of local builders. The cost has been quite reasonable and they have all worked very well.

If an indoor riding hall is possible so much the better, for here horse and rider (and coach!) can work unhindered, in comfort, and under consistent conditions. But here again it is not necessary to go to the vast expense of building one as most commercial equestrian centres will hire out their indoor facilities by the hour. Both the all-weather arena and the indoor arena are the gymnasiums of jumping training. In these the really concentrated work is done to bring the horse to his peak as a jumper.

You must always keep in mind, however, that variety is the spice of life. We want the jumping horse to be 100 per cent obedient, by all means, but what we do not want is a brain-washed jumping machine. So we mix up the daily routine in the 'gymnasium' with some long, relaxed walks around your own paddock or along bridle-paths or around the fields of a neighbouring farmer. Nowadays, in my opinion, a quiet ride around the roads and lanes is a thing of the past. Country roads, with an almost year-round flow of huge tractors and trailers, giant bulk grain lorries and massive combine harvesters, are not the place for even the most traffic-proof horse or pony. The risks are just far too great. But most farmers will let you exercise around the edges of their fields – do stick to the edges or you will soon find that the privilege is withdrawn. Remember it is his livelihood you might be damaging.

On these relaxation days let your showjumper relax – let him be just what he is – a natural outdoor animal. In other words let him just be a horse again. Ride out on as free a rein as you can so that the horse can have a look around at the rest of the world. Give him nice, long, slow cantering and jogging on a loose rein and when the conditions are right let him have a nice 'breeze-up' at a strong pace. The intensive training days keep the showjumper hard, fit, supple

and mentally sharp but these relaxation days are good for him mentally and physically . . . and they are good for you too!

In the afternoons, weather permitting, let your showjumper out in the paddock for a few hours grazing. We keep horses shut up in loose boxes and stalls far too much during the day. A sporting horse under intensive training is like the university student. When he is working the world is serious but when he is not then let him relax and be himself.

It is not, therefore, vital to have an expensive all-weather schooling ring, an indoor school or acres of rolling paddocks, to produce your own showjumper at home.

PRACTICE FENCES

Once you have the schooling area sorted out the next step is some practice fences. But before going on to discuss the aims of practice fences let's just take a look at the fences themselves. Again a fortune does not have to be spent on a full set of show fences but, even if you start off with just one fence it must be of the best quality. There are no cheap methods or short-cuts that can help either the horse or the rider to get ready for competition showjumping at any level. A flimsy branch stuck between two tree-stumps is absolutely useless for schooling a showjumper and a sheep hurdle in front of a hedge just as useless for the schooling of a cross-country horse. Equally, believe it or not (I have actually seen this tried) sheets of corrugated iron pegged to the ground on the landing side of a fence will not produce a confident water jumper!

The British Show Jumping Association runs a jump store where it sells second-hand jumps which have been used on the show circuit. I have always found this is the best way of putting together a good set of show fences for schooling at home. They are solid and properly made although they may need some repainting. They are, however, very heavy to move around but then it should keep you fit for your riding!

To start off with, in the early days of your schooling programme, half a dozen cavalletti will do the job as well as any show fences. These very simple movable frames can form, by placing one on top of the other, the basic shape of show fence – the upright and the spread. Cavalletti are invaluable for the schooling of young horses and the education of the rider. The traditional cavalletti are made of a solid wooden pole of 9ft (2.75m) bolted to a stout 'X' frame. These X-frames are set just off the right angle so that by merely turning the cavalletti over three different heights can be achieved . . . 10in (25cm), 15in (38cm) and 19in (48cm). Because of the simple design of the X-frames the cavalletti can be placed on top of each other to make schooling fences such as oxers, parallel bars and verticals. There are many on the market made from synthetic materials, making them lighter to move around and easier to look after, and this is one area where we can save ourselves a little bit of money . . . and any horse-owner, amateur or professional, would be foolish to overlook the opportunity.

Old rubber tyres make good, and safe supports for jumping rails which can be used when setting out a working grid. Railway sleepers,

The object of practice fences at home is to improve the horse's jumping technique and obedience, with the ultimate aim of preparing horse and rider for the competition arena. Here we can quite clearly see the horse measuring his distance from the groundline upwards, even to a simple cross rails

Two simple practice fences set out in the paddock. The spread has been given extra depth by a slanted front rail, and the vertical has its cross rail sloping towards the direction from the which the horse will be approaching. A simple but effective method of giving fences at home a little bit of variety in style

which can be bought quite cheaply, can also be used in this way. I also find these, by the way, very useful as border markers for a schooling arena. So you can get two uses from your jumping rails which may not save a fortune but will at least leave a few pennies that can be spent elsewhere. Having put together the raw materials the next step is to put them to use.

The aim of practice fences is threefold:

1 To improve the horse's style, confidence and technique over fences.
2 To improve the rider's style and technique.
3 To prepare horse and rider for the competition arena.

The fences therefore must be designed and laid out to achieve these objectives. Whether you make your own fences or buy a set of schooling fences will depend on how much you can spend but the following points should be kept in mind:

1 Variety is the most important factor and this can be achieved by working over the two basic types of show fence – the vertical and the spread. For example, a brush fence or a jump 'filler' on their own will make simple verticals but placed in front of some low rails they make a spread. As your horse progresses you can make a gate, planks, a narrow stile, dig out some dry ditches and water ditches and eventually get enough jump material together to be able to construct a double and treble combination. Try to mix in some rustic rails with the coloured ones.
2 Do not site the fences in a circle or uniform layout but try to position them so there are at least two changes of rein on the approaches and plan at least two fences which can be jumped from both directions.
3 You should always have somebody working with you on the ground, preferably your jumping coach, if not, a friend or a parent. Nothing will defeat the object of a schooling session more than a rider continually getting on and off a young horse to put rails back up or to change fences. This is also a safety pre-caution, never school over fences on your own. Accidents in showjumping are rare but they can happen!
4 The type of ground you put your fences on is just as important as the siting of them. The 'going' or 'footing' (the state of the ground) must be the best possible. Heavy, wet or sticky going

could frighten a young horse or, worse still for a showjumper, encourage him to be careless in his jumping. In other words the amount of energy and concentration that a horse has to put in because of the 'pull' of the heavy going is in relation to the results he can give. Jumpers, just like racehorses, favour a certain type of footing. Some like it soft, some like it with just a bit of give in the ground, others like it hard and some like it very soft. But in schooling the novice jumper we have to try to avoid conditions that make jumping more difficult or complicated. Later when the horse is 'made' he will tell you what type of footing he likes or dislikes.

Obviously very few horse-owners can have the perfect piece of ground for schooling at home and even fewer can guarantee it. This is an everyday problem for most trainers and horse-owners but it can be overcome or at the least controlled with simple straight-forward management. For example, moving the fences in a systematic rotation from week to week will help considerably. Jumping horses tend to 'poach' the take-off and landing side of fences only, so by moving the fences around it is possible to keep this problem under control. In very wet weather it may be necessary to move the fences every day which makes the whole thing sound like a full-time job! But once you take a horse or pony into your family . . . it is a full-time job for somebody!

5 The horse measures his fences from the bottom. That is to say he measures his distances from the fence, his point of take-off, from ground level upwards so any way that the base of the fence can be made clear or obvious will give the horse confidence. All schooling fences should have a clear ground-line. This can be achieved in a number of ways, for example, you can place a pole, either white or brightly coloured, along the base of the fence or place a small brush fence in front of the jump or, again, a small simulated wall, and so on. Never use oil-drums or straw bales! I've seen more accidents with horses, ponies and riders put off jumping for the rest of their lives through the use of these than anything else. Use oil-drums or straw bales as wings to fences by all means but never as material to build a fence. Only with the experienced jumper can a clearly defined ground-line be left out.

6 Schooling fences should be kept between 2ft 6in to 3ft 6in (76cm to 1.05m) for a novice horse and something like 2ft 9in to 4ft (84cm to 1.20m) for the more experienced jumper.

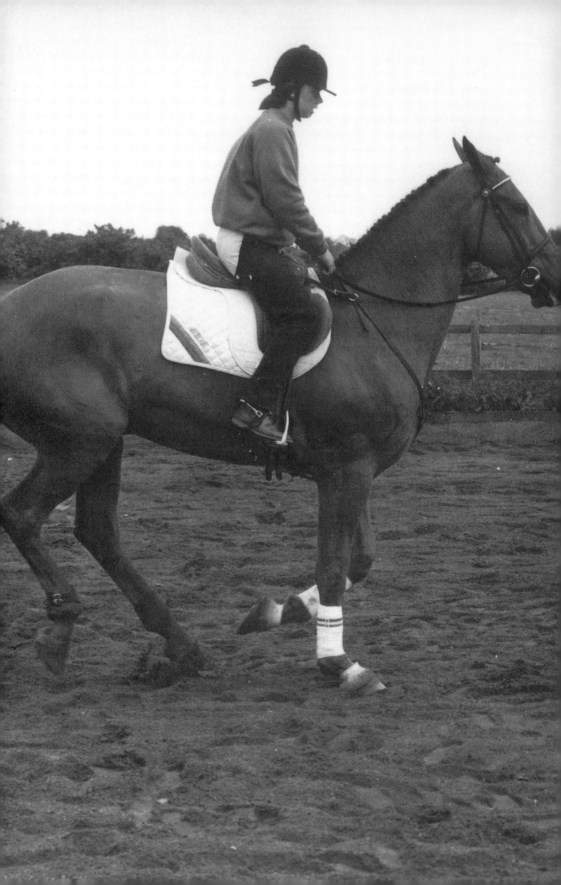

An obvious base line to a simple practice fence has helped the horse to come in deeper, as if the small cross rails were a 3ft 6in show fence

7 It is of more value, in the training and warming–up sense, to increase the width of spread practice fences rather than the height. There are two reasons for this: firstly, it encourages the novice horse – and an experienced one for that matter – to use his body correctly over a fence and, secondly, it 'warms–up' the rider to go with the movement of the horse. In the early stages this can be done by quite simply placing a pole on the ground in front of a small vertical and placing another behind it. Both rails should be some 3ft (90cm) away from the actual rail which is to be jumped thus forming a pyramid shape.

8 Try to make schooling fences look inviting by keeping the rails as clean and bright as circumstances will allow. Try not to use split or chipped rails. Make the wings look part of the fence as much as is possible.

9 Erect some fences that you can see through but are not flimsy.

Jumping Lane

If you have the space a jumping lane is useful for work under saddle in the early days of schooling. Try and site it in a wind-protected area, preferably with a natural enclosure to one side like a hedgerow, wall or bank and down the other side put up some simple posts and rails. The fences in the jumping lane or chute should ideally number about six to seven and keep them quite low and natural-looking with a mixture of verticals and spreads. I always use a jumping chute for introducing novice horses (and riders) to some of the 'funnies' we now see in showjumping, even at novice level, like dry ditches, water ditches and banks. But all the obstacles in the chute should be set on even strides, that is to say about 12ft (3.65m) for the non-jumping stride of the average horse. Certainly mix them up, however, using a three-stride distance, a four-stride distance, a two-stride distance etc.

The advantages of a jumping lane are twofold: firstly, it improves the technique and balance of the rider and, secondly, it encourages confidence, suppleness and quick reflexes in the horse. How can these two advantages be put to the best use?

IMPROVING THE RIDER'S TECHNIQUE

Because the horse is enclosed in the jumping lane once he has entered it the rider can relax and concentrate on purely riding forward and on maintaining a good rhythm as the fences come along in a regulated sequence.

56

ENCOURAGING SUPPLENESS AND QUICK REFLEXES

This is an area which is so often neglected in riding training. No matter how perfectly the rider may perform according to some book or manual it is essential that the rider is at least as fit and agile as his horse. There are two simple exercises that can be carried out with safety if a jumping lane is available. The first is to take the stirrup leathers off the saddle completely and then ride down the jumping lane.

The second is to take the saddle off completely and ride down the lane bareback. Both, as I say, simple little exercises that can bring that vital ingredient into learning . . . fun!

TACK AND EQUIPMENT

So much for facilities, now we are going to look at some of the specialised equipment we are going to use before going on to the work in earnest. These are the tools of the trade designed to help the horse's technique, the rider's control and position, and, in some cases, as precautionary measures for the knocks and bumps that will happen in all training programmes.

Boots and Guards

When working young horses I like to have a pair of knee-guards on them in the early days and most certainly tendon boots for all schooling and exercise sessions. Whether you put boots on behind, like brushing boots, will depend on the action of the horse. Some horses move closely behind and, particularly when shod all round, tend to knock their hind leg-joints. Brushing boots are the best safeguard against this although in many cases the horse can be shod in such a way that he does not knock himself. If conditions are right and the footing is good I have often not shod young horses behind until they are almost ready to show.

Over-reach boots in front are essential because it is so easy for jumping horses, novices or made ones, to strike into a front heel with a hind toe and this can often cause serious lameness.

The Saddle

What type of saddle you will use may be a matter of taste and comfort but a simple jumping saddle with knee rolls, and not thigh rolls, is generally the best. Thigh rolls tend to force a rider into a fixed and unnatural position. The less padding there is under the

Whether you use brushing boots on your horse's hindlegs will depend on how close he moves behind. But any protection of a horse's joints during training is probably worth it, and here we can see how the brushing boots protect the lower joints of the hindlegs

(left)
Prevention is better than cure – in all schooling sessions keep your horse as well protected as you can from the day-to-day knocks which are part and parcel of any sporting training programme. Here Rollo is fitted with front tendon bandages, but tendon boots would give the same protection. Much of this equipment, thanks to modern materials, is now quick and easy to put on and remove, as well to keep clean

Over-reach boots in jumping training and flatwork are, in my opinion, essential. Much of the work we do in jumping training involves the lengthening and shortening of the horse's stride, so there is always the risk that a young horse will over-step with his hindfeet and strike into the heels of his front feet. Over-reach boots are even more essential when competing in the show arena

59

saddle flap the better for jumping because the rider will get more 'feel' of his horse and, in turn the horse will get more 'feel' of the rider.

The Bridle

The bridle is another matter altogether. For some this too seems to be a question of taste but it should not be! Most young horses, if they have been mouthed and handled correctly in their formative years should have no need for anything but the simple, straight-forward snaffle bridle. Those to be recommended are the egg-butt and the D-ring. Both are less likely to pinch or burn the horse's lips or the corners of his mouth. The thing to remember about bits of all kinds is that the thinner the mouthpiece the more severe its action on the bars of the horse's mouth and the thicker the mouthpiece the softer the action. Even a simple, uncomplicated bit like a snaffle, if thin in the mouthpiece, can be an instrument of considerable severity if used forcefully or incorrectly.

The dropped-noseband is a useful and effective piece of equipment in jumping, and not just in early schooling work but throughout the horse's competitive career. The dropped-noseband should only be used with a snaffle bridle and it serves as an aid or back-up to it. It encourages the horse to accept the bit and to give to it by putting the horse into a situation where he will more easily understand that stiffening his lower jaw is a resistance to the bridle. The trouble with this type of equipment is that too many riders see it as a way of dominating the horse rather than a means of improving the horse as a ride but most equipment at our disposal has this drawback in the wrong hands. In the end nothing is an effective substitute for good riding and training, some short-cuts will get temporary results but never consistent or satisfying ones.

The dropped-noseband should be fitted so that it does not interfere with the horse's nostrils or breathing. The back section passes below the bit and under the jaw. It should not be so tight that the horse cannot move his lips but just enough to stop him from opening his mouth. It is this pressure, under the groove of the chin, which encourages the horse to go with a relaxed jaw. In other words, the horse gives little or no resistance to the rider's hands. No martingale of any sort should be fitted to a dropped noseband.

Martingales

There are many forms of martingales such as running martingales, standing martingales and so on but like many bits they are not a means of control. They are merely an artificial aid to a finer control in certain aspects of the sport. If a young horse has been handled well through his early education there should be no need for any sort of martingale. But, of course, we are not always presented with the perfect situation. Often you cannot have untouched young horses to train or to ride. It is more the rule than the exception that by the time the horse we have in our hands has reached a certain age he will have received some form of training, good or mediocre, which has influenced his character. In these circumstances it's not unusual that a martingale may be needed sometimes just quite simply for rider control and others because the horse is so used to it that it has become a form of security.

Horses can become used to certain items of tack and any sudden changes can confuse them. There are only two ways around this: either retrain the horse to a simpler system or let the horse go on as before in the hope that certain things can be gradually phased out. With the increasing costs of keeping horses the latter is perhaps the more practical of the two but much will depend on the time available, the resources at the trainer's and owner's disposal and the natural abilities of both the horse and the rider.

In any study of artificial aids, such as martingales and supplementary equipment, the conformation of the horse and the aptitude of the rider are directly related to these extras and their place in the training of showjumpers. The conformation of a horse is one of the governing factors in this respect. Let me give an example: a horse which is thick in the jugular groove, in other words the base of the neck and under the throat area, will find it physically uncomfortable to bend from the poll. In this case the running martingale fitted correctly will improve the horse as a ride by acting as a support to the bridle.

It is not unusual for professional riders to fit a short running martingale to this type of horse and by doing so get that horse to jump accurately if not correctly. The professional often has no option as

(pp 62-3)
Our model, Rollo, ready for action. The saddle is not too bulky and fits nicely into his back. His joints are protected and because he has had good basic training he needs neither a martingale nor a drop-noseband. But notice that he is fitted with a breast girth – his wither is rather low and flat so there is a danger of the saddle moving back on him during work or competition. So, again, it is the tried and tested philosophy of prevention is far better than cure

he has to get his horse going quickly and winning classes. It is not always crude or cruel to use artificial aids in this way providing it is in expert hands. What is cruel is to copy these methods without the ability to carry them out. Another situation where martingales can be justified is in retraining of both horse and rider. The running martingale can be a very efficient piece of equipment as a transitional schooling aid. For example, a horse of not too perfect conformation (and like us there are quite a few of them, not every horse can be beautifully made), such as with too long a back or too short a neck, can have problems in finding true balance when carrying a rider. He would obviously have no problems when unridden. Because of some defect in his make or shape such a horse will find it difficult or even uncomfortable to come into the shortened form for true collection. Equally the rider may find that he is getting frustrated because he is working away at something that cannot be completely attained. The leverage of a running martingale can help to keep the horse in a 'rounded' form without the rider interfering with the horse's mouth. Riders, like horses, have not always got everything in perfect balance and the martingale can give them a measure of control which leads to confidence and confidence leads to a better performance.

Draw-reins

In today's modern training yard draw-reins have become a common sight although they have existed in dealers' yards for many years. It was, perhaps, the German showjumping riders who popularised them throughout Europe and North America. The basis of all young German riders' equestrian education is and always has been, dressage. Their natural understanding of correct flat-work accounts for much of their success in the sport of showjumping. There are many who say the Germans have an ugly style. They dominate their horses. But if you watch them closely you will see that the majority of them have a very sensitive touch with their horses. They expect and get complete obedience to the bridle.

Draw-reins, although not a new idea, are an accepted everyday artificial aid used in the training of all riding horses, not just potential jumpers. But they are just that – an aid which encourages the horse to be soft to his bridle and obedient to the rider, without forcing him to give his mouth or be put into a position where he will pull against the rider's hands

The draw-rein should run through the bottom, and weakest, part of the rider's hands

Here Addie and Rollo demonstrate quite clearly the use and benefits of the draw-rein in action. The horse is not resisting the bridle; the rider is not pulling the horse's head down low or bent. The horse is active in his hindlegs, balanced in his stride and we can see the muscles of his neck, shoulder, forearm and croup being worked at the same time

On a jumping course in a competition if they ask their horse to come back to them, in other words shorten, the horse understands, does it immediately and smoothly. Equally if they ask their horse to go away from them, lengthen, they get the same immediate response.

This, in a nutshell, is what draw-rein work is all about. They are an aid to encourage the horse to be responsive to the rider. We will be discussing all this in more detail later but we can sum up the use of draw-reins as:

1 An aid to be used with the legs and seat to build muscle with suppleness, balance with smoothness and willing submission to the bridle.

2 They are not a piece of equipment for forcing the horse to carry his head and neck in a certain position. If used in that way they have the negative effect of destroying the traction of the hind legs and making the horse's mouth hard (insensitive).

CHAPTER 4

Feeding for Fitness

Daily diet is as important to the competition horse as it is to any human athlete. The better and more correct his diet, the better he will feel, look and perform. That might be stating the obvious to some of you but it still never fails to amaze me the number of ponies and horses one sees in the show ring that are not in a fit or healthy condition. Their coats are dull, their skins tight and they have a generally stale look about them.

SIGNS OF HEALTH

Let's start by looking at the healthy horse and working back to the manger. What are the signs of health in the horse?

- Head alert, eyes wide open and taking an interest in what is going on around him. Ears moving to and fro. The Americans have a great saying: 'the healthy, fit horse, has the look of eagles'.
- The horse 'clears up' all his feed and drinks regularly.
- The inside lining of the eyes – which can be pulled down gently with the index finger and thumb – and the inner skin of the nostrils is salmon-pink in colour.
- The skin can be 'lifted', by the forefinger and thumb from the ribs beneath it and the coat is smooth, bright and glossy in appearance.
- The horse stands with his bodyweight evenly distributed on all four feet. It is quite normal and natural for horses to rest a hind leg occasionally but if he rests a foreleg then it is a sign that the leg or shoulder is worrying him. Pointing one of the front toes, except when grazing or eating, can also be a sign of leg trouble.
- Urine should be clear to light yellow in colour and a healthy horse will pass droppings about eight times a day.
- The normal temperature of a horse is 100.5°F or 38°C and his normal respiratory rate at rest is 10–12 to the minute.

69

DIET AND ROUTINE

The secret to a healthy daily feeding programme is based on one simple rule: be consistent in feeding times. It doesn't matter a great deal what times you feed at, within reason, as long as it is the same time each day. Horses thrive on routine. The objective should be to keep the feeding programme as near to the horse's natural feeding method as we can get. In other words as the horse is by nature a grazing animal we will get better results by feeding little and often.

The feeding of competition horses is quite an art. It is not enough just to put feed in the manger or hay in the haynet and let the animal get on with it. The owner or trainer must make a study of the horse by watching him at feed times and looking at him carefully each day. If the horse clears-up at every feed, and particularly if he licks every last morsel out of the manger, then you can be certain you are giving the right diet and the food he likes! If you watch your horse enough he will tell you when you have got it right.

Try to put a few minutes aside each day to have a good look at your horse. Study him. Is he showing the signs of health we have just listed? Is he putting on more muscle or more fat? Bulk foods such as hay, bran and grass etc, put on fat. Concentrates like oats, improve muscle. Linseed encourages a glossy coat and healthy skin. So it's all a bit of a mixture of 'eye' and commonsense for the horse-owner. Husbandry in all its forms has always been an art and quite a lot of science but feeding the competition horse can be brought down to ten basic rules!

1 Keep the feeding programme as near to the horse's natural feeding habits as possible – feed little and often.
2 Feed plenty of bulk food such as hay. This will act as a substitute for natural grazing by keeping the digestive system well filled. The horse's digestive processes, which are quite delicate for such a big animal, will not remain balanced without adequate bulk.
3 Keep feed measures in relation to the work done. For example, increase the concentrated high-protein foods, such as oats, when the horse is in 'hard' work and decrease them when he is in 'light' work. (Hard work would be regular schooling every day with competing in the ring two or three times a week. Light work would be general exercise with no competing.) But if you have a horse on the sick list or roughed-off (resting) then don't

feed any concentrates (or very little anyway) but increase the bulk foods.

4 Do not make any sudden changes in the diet. These should be introduced gradually and spread over several days.

5 Try to be consistent in daily feeding times. Horses thrive on routine. They seem to have a clock in their heads when it comes to feed times. I don't think they are all that bothered what actual time it is as long as each feed comes along at the same time each day. The same with exercising and schooling. They will progress more quickly if they go out at the same time each day be it in the morning or in the evening providing it's every morning and every evening. This is why racehorses always look so well and so pleased with themselves when they pull out each morning. Everything in the racing yard, stable management and training, is run to a definite daily routine and timetable.

6 Feed only good and clean forage. Cheap foodstuffs are a false economy especially cheap hay.

7 Try to feed something tasty each day, for example, some sliced (not chopped) carrots or apples. In spring or summertime put an armful of cut grass into his box but *never* lawn-mower cuttings. Horses find these difficult to masticate and if the cuttings ball up, and they always do, the horse can choke.

8 Never ask a horse to do any fast or hard work after a big feed or when his stomach is full of grass. This can cause irreparable damage because the stomach lies next to the chest and, if full, will press on the lungs and damage the horse's wind as well as increasing the likelihood of colic.

9 Always check that your horse is drinking regularly and not just after working but throughout the whole day.

10 Always have a block or slab of rock salt in your horse's manger or on the floor of his box. Horses will spend hours licking away at rock salt and it will encourage regular drinking. If this is not possible then add a good soupspoon of salt to at least one feed per day. Water is essential not only to the digestive system but also to clear undigested food that may be in the stomach.

Feeding programmes in books can only be general suggestions but the following guide-lines will give you a sound basis to your own feeding programme.

CONCENTRATED FOODS

Oats

These are a balanced, nutritional and readily digested food on which horses do well. They can be fed either crushed, bruised or rolled but crushed oats can be over-crushed resulting in the loss of the floury content of the oat which is its protein and feed value. I prefer the halfway house of bruised oats. Whole oats are not very economical as a large percentage of them seems to go straight through the horse's body!

The difference in nutritional value between black or white oats, by the way, is very small but both varieties must be plump and clean when fed in. Never use musty or dusty oats – you will soon see your vet's bills going up if you do! Oats are an energy-producing food so care must be taken when giving them to small ponies or horses which are not in regular work. In most cases they are better off without them.

Suggested measures for feeding oats:

A competition horse standing, say, 15.1hh and upwards, in intensive training and regularly competing: 14lb (6.3kg) mixed in with the other ingredients and spread equally over the number of feeds given daily (three to four).

A competition pony, standing 14.2hh: 3-5lb (1.4-2.3kg) spread over two of the daily feeds given, preferably the evening or afternoon feed.

Barley and Flaked Maize

These are used as concentrates in many countries with success but flaked maize does have a tendency to overheat the blood. Barley, if boiled, is a good pick-me-up for a tired horse after a competition and for sick horses. It's also very effective for tempting shy or delicate feeders. The main value of barley (uncooked) and flaked maize is that they can both add variety to the diet and they contain protein as well as fattening properties.

Suggested measures for feeding when given to a horse in serious training are about 3-4lb (1.4-1.8kg) per day spread over several feeds. Again use them as variety – flaked maize one week, barley the next and so on.

Beans

These are a highly nutritious food and bruised or split can be used in small amounts to give variety to the feed. By small amounts we are talking about a handful in, say, the evening or afternoon feed.

Horse and Pony Cubes

These are man-made compound concentrates which have become very popular with many horse-owners. In fact, there are so many brands on the market now ranging from those for the racehorse and competition horse through to the summer holiday Pony Club pony. Most of them are made from a mixture of oats, bran, maize, barley, locust bean, linseed cake, groundnut meal, grass meal and molasses with vitamin and minerals added.

The main advantage of these compound feeds is that they are labour-saving in so much as they do not need premixing and storage is easier. Most horses and ponies certainly seem to like them but I prefer to know exactly what and how much I am putting into my horse. These compounds are a bit like fast foods. They are useful, though, in adding variety to the diet and can be used at the following relative rate: 1-1½lb (.5-.7kg) of cubes replacing 1lb (.5kg) of oats. They are more effective if fed with bran and/or chaff as this helps mastication and salivation before swallowing. Most of the large companies have feed consultants who can be very helpful in advising private owners on feeding programmes.

Mineral and Vitamin Additives

There are, again, many brands on the market, some good, some bad, some indifferent. However, a scientifically balanced vitamin/mineral compound is an essential for a horse in hard training and regularly competing. Before you decide which one you are going to use do seek the advice of your veterinary surgeon.

Grass and Hay

There are two main bulk feeds natural to the horse: they are grass and hay. The horse or pony kept at grass obviously feeds himself as far as bulk foods are concerned. But for the stabled horse hay is the substitute for grass and should therefore be available to him at almost any time of the day or night.

Good hay should be sweet-smelling and fibrous. There are five types best suited for horses: sainfoin (the most nutritious), rye grass, trefoil, meadow and clover mixture, which contains clovers, rye grass, with either trefoil or meadow. Clover hay is rich but it must be of good quality. The poorer grades tend to be dusty, mouldy and wasteful. I find mixture hay with more rye grass than clover the best general-purpose bulk feed. New hay, by the way, that is less than, say, six months old should not be fed to horses or ponies. It can cause severe digestive problems.

Chaff

This is simply chopped hay but it is an essential component to a balanced feeding programme. Chaff adds bulk to the daily feeds and encourages good mastication but, once more, it must be of good quality made from the higher grades of hay.

Oat straw chopped up with hay is a useful bulk feed for horses and ponies which are out of training or roughed-off.

OTHER FEEDSTUFFS

Bran

This is the refuse of grain and aids digestion of the daily feeds but fed dry it can be constipating and fed in too large quantities it will dull the horse's coat. Fed damp it is useful as a mild laxative. From 4 to 5lb (1.8 to 2.25kg) is about right as a daily ration for a competition horse. I always dampen feeds with a little hot water on top of the bran before mixing the feeds. It gives the feed an attractive smell. A bran mash should be fed to a competition horse once a week, preferably the night before his day off.

Making a bran mash is quite simple. First fill a feed bucket about two-thirds full of bran then pour on boiling water. Stir the two up until all the bran is thoroughly wet. Then cover the bucket with a sack and allow to stand until the mash is cool enough to feed in. The end-product should be 'crumble-dry', add a little salt and a handful of oats and you have a very tempting bran mash.

Linseed

This is the seed of the flax plant and it encourages a glossy coat while helping conditioning. Linseed can be used in two forms, as a jelly or as a tea. Add a feedbowl of linseed to your horse's evening feed two or three times a week and you will soon see your horse glow.

LINSEED JELLY

Allow 1lb (.5kg) of uncooked linseed for each feed, ie, to make enough for four feeds use 4lb (1.8kg) of linseed. Place the linseed in a large saucepan. Cover with water and leave to stand overnight with the lid on. Add more water and place on a slow steady burner. If you are lucky enough to have an Aga or range oven then put it in the cool oven. Leave it to come slowly to the boil. Linseed must be boiled, by the way, as in any other condition it can be poisonous. If your cooking has been a success the linseed will have set like a jelly. Leave to cool and you have a linseed jelly to feed in with the evening feed.

LINSEED TEA

Prepare in exactly the same way as for a jelly but keep adding water so that the linseed does not solidify. The water in which the linseed has boiled has a very high nutritional content and horses seem to love it mixed in with a feed.

Root Crops

Succulent foods such as root crops are very useful for adding variety to the daily feed programme. Such crops are carrots, swedes, mangolds, turnips, beetroots and parsnips. They must be scrubbed clean in warm water and sliced. Chopped root crops can become trapped in the throat. Sliced carrots are the most popular with horses although I had a young German horse at one time and he didn't know what they were! It was weeks before we could get him to eat them. Measures are not all that important but start off with 1lb (.5kg) per day and build up to 2lb (1kg) a day.

Finally, and this should go without saying but many people seem to overlook it, do thoroughly clean all feed buckets and utensils *every* time you use them *and* wash out your horse's manger at least three times a week. Even the best forage in the world will not be appetising from a stale-smelling bucket or manger. I much prefer to feed my horses and ponies in buckets or vulcanised rubber feed containers. If you watch a horse out grazing he puts his head down to eat, and he will very rarely eat herbage or leaves which are above his head. So why not stick to his natural style of eating when he is stabled by putting his food in a container on the floor? It seems to work and horses seem happier eating that way.

SUGGESTED DAILY FEEDING ROUTINE

07.30
Fresh water and first feed. After riding out put up a small hay net and freshen up the water.
12.00
Second feed, freshen up the water and put up a full hay net.
16.30–17.00
Third feed, freshen bucket of water and put up a small hay net.
20.00–20.30
Fourth feed, freshen up the water and put up a full hay net.

CHAPTER 5

Fitness and Groundwork

The first aspect in getting a jumping horse fit which a private owner has to consider is the difference between work and exercise. This difference is perhaps narrow but nonetheless it exists and it is important. Basically it amounts to this: exercise is concerned with improving and hardening muscles while keeping unwanted fat off the conditioned body, 'exercising' the lungs (wind) and the heart (circulation). Work is schooling (education) and preparation for a specific job through improving suppleness, balance and mental alertness. Both should be directly related to the diet and age of the horse, for example, bringing an experienced horse up to competition fitness will be easier than bringing a young novice horse to the same mental and physical state.

Weather conditions will, of course, affect the planning and progress of the work/exercise programme unless an indoor school is available. But the horse is by nature an outdoor creature and quite capable of coping with the normal seasonal weather conditions providing he is fit and healthy. Too much work indoors can give a false picture of just how fit he is. Too much schooling indoors can also lead to a false situation as most horses will learn quickly when indoors as there are few distractions or problems to affect their concentration. So if an indoor school is available use it prudently, balancing the training hours between work outside and work under cover. The object of exercise is to make and maintain condition. The programme, therefore, should be planned to build up progressively, starting off with a short period each day at a slow pace, ie plenty of active walking and slow trotting over fairly flat terrain.

EXERCISE REGIME

As the horse gets fitter so the exercise periods and their pace can be increased. It's not difficult to judge the horse's progress towards fitness. His eyes will look brighter and more alert, muscles can be

Lack of physical condition and general fitness can often be the cause of problems in the warm-up before a competition or in the arena. Situations like these are not always rider or horse error: they can often be caused by the stiffness of the horse in his body-muscles, and the lack of concentration in his mind

seen developing on his neck, shoulders, forearm and hindquarters. His skin and coat will get a bloom about them but one of the easiest signs to read is the rhythm of his breathing. As the horse gets 'harder' he will blow less and breathe with an even and effortless rhythm.

The aim at the outset of exercise is to work off any fat that the horse is carrying from his 'soft' condition. This can only be done gradually as any stress or demanding exercise done when the horse is carrying too much weight can do irreparable damage to his wind and heart. It is, of course, impossible to lay down hard-and-fast rules or principles governing time or number of weeks needed to get a jumping horse fit. Horses, like us, vary considerably in how much exercise they need or how long it will take to get into a hard condition, so a good measure of commonsense is needed in interpreting any guide-lines. But we can generalise to a certain degree.

Each exercise period should start with at least fifteen to twenty minutes free walking and finish with about the same period also at the walk. The initial walking period helps the horse to get rid of any stiffness after a long night in his loose-box and it gives him a chance to have a look around him and settle down. The returning walk helps him to relax after exercise and in the summer to cool off before returning to the yard or barn.

The actual exercise period can start at around forty-five minutes per day building up to one and a half to possibly two hours a day. One day of the week should be set aside as a rest day. This is often useful for arranging attention from the farrier and, if you have the facility, turn your horse out for a few hours of freedom. If you haven't, try and find the time to lead him out for a bite of grass. Too many horse-owners leave their horses in loose boxes for hours on end. Horses soon get bored and a fit horse will become bored much more quickly!

The aim of your programme is to build up to steady exercise at a consistent pace and rhythm in the walk, trot and canter. Let your horse have as much freedom as possible especially of his head and neck. We don't need a high degree of collection while out at exercise. As soon as the horse is showing the signs of his fitness developing bring in some uphill and downhill exercise. Slow regulated trotting up a slope or hill builds muscle particularly in the hindquarters, forearm and thigh. Walking, on as free a rein as possible, downhill encourages balance and builds the muscles of the neck, shoulder, forearm and back. Fast exercise like galloping and extended cantering will 'clean' the horse's wind (and yours!) especially on a nice bright, sharp and frosty morning . . . there is nothing quite like it for both of you.

The exercise programme and the work schedule can be co-ordinated to add variety to your horse's daily routine. Try following a long exercise period with a short schooling session and vice versa, or one day the exercise period can be dropped and replaced by an intensive work session. Regularity is the basis of any athlete's approach to peak condition but boredom and staleness will only result in frustrating results.

The object of work is to educate and prepare the horse mentally and physically for a specific type of competition. A dressage horse would be worked to a dressage programme: suppling exercises; learning new movements and improving his responses to the aids of the rider. An event- or horse-trials competition horse would be worked through his dressage, cross-country jumping or showjumping and his exercise programme would be geared to stamina. With the showjumping horse there is a subtle difference in that we not only work him on the flat but we also set out to keep improving his technique over fences. The margin of error in showjumping, at any level, is very narrow. Basically it's one fence down and you will be lucky if you make the line-up at presentation time. Although we require the jumping horse to be obedient and willing at all times, it will be self-defeating if he is turned into some sort of four-legged machine. Remember that saying of Fred Broome Senior's: '. . . always leave 20 per cent to the horse'.

WORK ON THE FLAT

So much for getting the horse fit for jumping, now we must take a look at the serious work on the flat and link that directly to training over fences. The three aims of our groundwork schooling will be:

1 Balance – both of horse and rider
2 Control and obedience (dressage)
3 Suppleness and rhythm

We must go back to your original equitation classes and take a longer look at collection, perhaps the most difficult and complicated aspect of competition riding which both horse and rider must understand, control, create and know. Without correct collection horse and rider will never show over fences with good consistent results.

To understand collection we can, to a certain degree, liken the horse to the motor car. Two more different locomotive vehicles might be difficult to find but we can use the principle of the motor car to give us a graphic example of the theory of collection we need from the jumping horse.

When the gearbox of a car is in neutral and the accelerator is not touched, the power unit is producing practically no energy and the vehicle will move neither backwards nor forwards. But if the gearbox is engaged the power unit will produce energy according to the amount of accelerator used, and that energy is of course, controlled by the driver. When the horse is in a state of collection, his hindquarters (the engine) are engaged for producing energy and the rider, by using his open or closed hand, his seat and leg aids, (the rider's accelerator) can control the amount of energy used. The relaxed horse, like the car in neutral, is not in a state of collection, is producing little or no energy and his hindquarters are not engaged. In other words *he* is in neutral.

Collection is defined as the concentration of the horse's energy when his body is in the shortened form on a light rein but a positive rein not a loose rein. When he has maximum control over his body and limbs through the extra activity of his hind legs he is in a position to respond immediately to his rider's aids. It is rather like the principle of the spring which is wound up to a shortened form to contain the energy force and then lengthened when that energy force is released. This is, perhaps, a more graphic example of what we are trying to achieve with the jumping horse. We have him wound up like a spring – collection – and we release that energy in varying degrees to get the power to jump a show fence. On landing we contain the energy again ready for the next obstacle.

I'm sure many of you have heard the well-used phrase in jumping circles: 'keep your horse's hocks under him'. A bit of an old-fashioned saying now as there is a lot more to modern showjumping than that, but basically it rings true. The horse is driven from behind, the hindquarters are his engine and his forward movement, whether it be on the flat or going into the air, is produced from behind the saddle. His forehand is his support and his head and neck are his balancing pole.

To concentrate the horse's energy (winding up the spring, if you like) the rider must encourage activity while controlling its output

Rollo has come into a nice state of collection at the canter. His hocks are well under him, he is making a nice round shape and there is little resistance to the bridle or the rider's rein hand

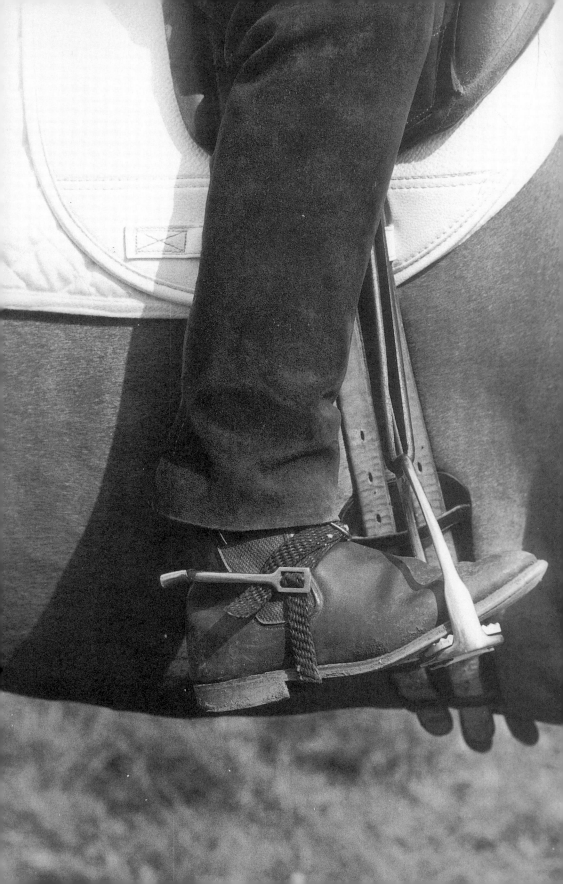

rate. This is done in such a way that the rider does not allow his weight to hinder the horse's natural support, the forehand. So there is no point in having the rider's weight being carried by the forehand as the ultimate goal of correct riding is to ride without hindering the horse's natural balance. The *total* weight of the rider must be evenly distributed in the middle of the saddle. The energy of the hind legs is created and encouraged by the squeezing of the rider's legs and the downward drive of his seat-bones . . . two of the most vital aids when approaching a fence.

AIDS

At this stage it might be worth taking a little time to remind ourselves what the rider's aids are and their function:

1 The hands control pace, direction, balance and feel.
2 The legs control pace, direction, balance and impulsion.
3 The seat controls impulsion, rhythm and balance.
4 The voice can encourage, calm or discourage according to tone.

The horse's energy is produced, controlled and then restricted by the rider's closed hands on the reins, *never* by pulling, once you start that the horse will start pulling and in the end he is going to win because he is the stronger. The closed hand says to the horse: 'the door is closed you must stay here,' and the open hand says: 'The door is open, through you go'. The energy which is contained by the closed hand pushes the horse's activity into an elevated attitude instead of a forward or backward attitude.

This is what is meant by bringing the horse's body into a shortened form: creating energy; bringing that energy to an elevated output and by releasing it or containing it at will, the rider has in effect lightened the whole body of the horse. If you watch a horse at liberty in a paddock you will see him actually doing this. When he wants a short stride he will elevate and shorten his body and when he wants to extend his stride he will flatten his body and lengthen

As every riding school pupil will know, the most regularly barked command is 'Keep your heels down!' For the jumping rider this must become natural, for the weight going down through the heel pulls the rider's seat deeper into the saddle. But the ankle should not be too rigid, for this is important to the jumping rider's position in the saddle: it is cushioned by the thighs, ankles and heels

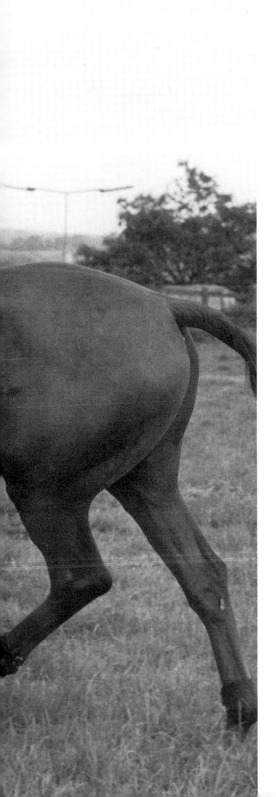

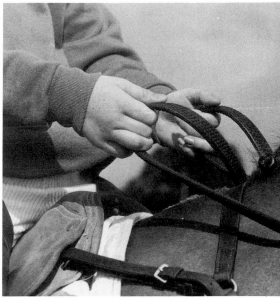

The hands control pace, direction, balance and, above all, feel. With the hands carried in this natural position, as if carrying two glasses of water, the rider has the flexibility to open the fingers and give to the horse, or close the fingers to contain the horse's energy or regulate his pace, without the temptation of pulling upwards or backwards

The total weight of the rider is evenly distributed in the middle of the horse and, as we can see here, the seat is deep with a close contact with the horse, yet relaxed and natural-looking

his stride. So collection really is bringing the horse to a natural state while carrying a rider and while listening to that rider's 'language' through the aids. When you achieve collection you will know it because the horse will give this marvellous feeling of being uphill. You will feel his entire front-end come up in front of you.

RHYTHM

Every horse has some sort of rhythm in his movement but the rider has to encourage the horse to move with a constant fluency. By doing so he is teaching the horse how to carry himself in a balanced manner and demonstrating to the horse his control over rhythm and therefore the power of the pace. It is no good just letting the horse go charging along at, say, a fast trot because the faster the horse's legs go without balance the less control the rider has over them. Whereas if the rider keeps the horse in a rhythmical, active trot he will have complete control over the horse's action at all times.

Why go to all this time and effort on the flat for a jumper? The answer to that is that we, the riders, walk the jumping course before a competition. The horse does not know when he enters the ring whether he is going to go left or right, or face a vertical fence, a spread fence or a combination of fences. (Mind you, I have seen some seasoned showjumping horses work out what sort of fences they are facing several strides before their rider does!) He must be under complete control and respond immediately to the rider's aids to tackle a showjumping course with accuracy.

Although we require the horse's action to be active we do not want to waste energy, so along with the activity the horse must be encouraged to move on a strong even stride. One of the best illustrations of this, for the rider, is the work at the trot but the principle is the same for all three paces. The rider 'asks' his horse to trot with a brisk action and a regular two-beat. (One beat for each diagonal, one diagonal being the near-fore and the off-hind and the other the off-fore and the near-hind.) Keeping a light but constant contact with the horse's mouth through the bridle the rider can then concentrate on the rhythm of the two-beat stride. If he feels the horse is breaking that steady two-beat rhythm, by slowing or quickening the pace, the rider can correct it. For instance, let's say the horse quickens his rhythm, the rider closes his lower legs against the horse, pushes down with his seat *but* closes his hands firmly. The

Rollo going in a nice even, well-balanced trot and here we can see quite clearly the diagonal of the two-beat rhythm. The near-hind is going forward with the off-hind, and the off-fore back with the near-hind. We can also see the perfect trot stride, with the off-hind about to step into the place left by the off-fore

horse then gives to the bridle and regulates his stride. If this is repeated each time the horse loses a constant rhythm it becomes a kind of self-demonstration to the horse and he will eventually settle into his 'gear' and trot on an even stride. This exercise can have a calming effect on free-going horses and can give impetus to horses with a lazy action but it does take patience and riding through.

The old saying in the horse world: 'No foot, no horse' can be extended to the phrase for showjumping: 'No mouth, no jumper'. But before an inexperienced rider can understand how to train his horse to submit to the bridle and have a correct head carriage, the rider has to understand why there is such a thing as correct head carriage.

The horse has been carrying his head around since the day he was born, so surely he knows best how it should be carried? Yes of course, the horse knows instinctively the best position to carry his head in to balance his body when he is free and loose but not with the added weight and movement of a rider placed on his back. The horse in a free state will alter his head and neck according to the pace or direction in which he is moving. At the gallop the head and neck are lowered and stretched out in front of the body, while at the trot the head comes up slightly and the neck changes into a shortened form. So when the horse is given the task of coping with the weight of the rider he has to be taught how to bring his balance in line with this. Once the rider is capable of feeling and maintaining balance then he can move on to teaching his horse to carry his head in such a position that the two 'moving-weight' factors can be related and controlled.

There are two traps the rider will at first fall into but they can easily be corrected. The first is the horse's head going too high when the rider asks for collection. Too high a head carriage will hollow the horse's back and in turn that will push the hindquarters out and away from the horse instead of being underneath him. In other words he will leave his hindquarters behind in his balance and movement. The second is the horse's head going too low which will encourage the horse to stiffen his jaw against the bridle and put him in the position where he can set his neck and forehand against the rider.

The only answer to both of these problems is to go back to square one and start again asking for collection until the horse understands what is being asked by the rider. In all training programmes, no matter how graduated, the important thing is to be satisfied with a little bit of improvement each time. To ask too much too soon of both horse and rider will only lead to confusion. In the case of the horse which persists in carrying his head too high through a fault of conformation or previous training and handling then the running martingale comes into its own as a justified and effective aid but do try and avoid going to the extreme of a standing martingale. This tends to encourage the horse to use the martingale as a second neck rather than help any improvement in the use of his muscle. Once used, the standing martingale is there for good; it is almost impossible to get rid of it.

The horse has been able to hollow his back and raise his head high, and in so doing set his body-weight against the rider and the bridle. Once in this position there is no point in the rider trying to haul the horse round. The depth of the rider's seat has been lost so there is no chance of using the outside leg, and the horse is 'running' away from the asking hand. The solution is to 'move the goal posts' by turning away to the left, circling, setting up and starting again

STIFF SIDE, SOFT SIDE

The majority of horses have a stiff side and a soft side to their mouths and their bodies rather like some people are left-handed and others right-handed. What has happened is that by favouring one side of his body or the other the horse has altered the balance of his muscle structure as far as we are concerned as riders and trainers. How does this come about? If you study horses at liberty you will see that they move slightly bent to one side. If that side is the left then because their bodies are bent – curved is most probably more accurate – to that direction then the muscles on that side will be in the shortened form all the time, and the muscles to the right side will be permanently kept in the lengthened form and vice

versa. This we can correct to bring the body into balance for a rider, to straighten the horse's action and at the same time take advantage of the situation to get the horse to give to the bridle.

To find out which side is the stiff or hard side ride your horse at the walk on a free rein. Then raise the left rein only and ask him to move to the left. If he responds immediately, with no resistance to

Addie working Rollo to his stiff side. We can see the resistance in his lower jaw as he tries to adjust to Addie's asking hand and bend his body around her inside leg aid. Next we see an entirely different picture. Rollo is relaxed, flexing to the bridle and accepting the inner leg aid. This is also another example of the use of draw-reins as an artificial aid: they are helping the horse and the rider without any pulling on the asking rein

the rein, and turns his head, neck and body in a curve to the directing rein then this is his soft side. Let him walk on again on a loose rein but this time take up the right rein only and once again ask him to move in that direction. If he resists, which he will do first with his jaw and then with his body, then this is his hard side. You will see this in the show ring quite often. A jumping horse will come round to, say, the right on a nice balanced curve but when going to the left the horse will lead from his shoulder with his head inclined away from the direction in which he has been asked to go.

Once we know the soft side and the hard side we can do something about it. The rider first gets his horse into a nice steady settled trot, even-paced and as relaxed as possible. The rider takes a firm contact on the left rein (we are assuming in this case the soft side is the left) and maintains that contact throughout the exercise. The rider's contact on the left rein should be even and constant but not in a pulling action. If the horse's soft side is the left then we will work in an anti-clockwise direction around the school or manège. If the soft side is his right we would obviously work on the other rein.

We now have our horse and rider trotting quietly around the arena. Once the horse has settled to the cadence of his trot the rider closes the fingers of his right hand in a squeezing action and raises the hand and rein at the same time. This raising action of the rein brings the pressure of the bit on the horse's lips and asks him to give his mouth to the stiff side. The rider will feel the give through the rein as the horse relaxes his jaw to his stiff side and he will also see the horse lower his head. The action of the right hand, like that of the left, must not be a backward motion but simply a firm squeeze through opening and closing the hand. It's rather like squeezing water out of a sponge slowly. This is an asking hand and should be backed up with the rider's leg aids to keep the forward impulsion. The system may not produce perfect results first time as the rider is in fact riding through the resistance of the stiff side. The 'asking' by the right hand should be repeated until the horse understands and gives to the rein.

This giving of the jaw can now be taken a stage further to transitions, one of the most important phases of flat training for the jumping horse. You will already know about basic transitions – going from trot to canter, canter to trot etc – but we are now going to extend the relaxing of the jaw into a dialogue between asking hand and asking leg during a transition.

Let's use coming from the trot to the walk as our exercise. The rider sits deep into the saddle, closes both legs to the horse and closes his hands in such a way as to resist without pulling. To make the reduction of pace smoother and more immediate the rider can now add a refinement to the transition. The rider resists more firmly with the right hand (stiff side) and puts just a bit more pressure on from his lower right leg so asking his horse to relax his jaw through the transition. If the horse's stiff side is the left then the asking aids will be the left hand and leg. The moment the rider feels the horse respond he relaxes his fingers and through his seat aid pushes the horse down into the walk. We have now got an 'asking and reward' dialogue going between the horse and the rider and it is *this* which is going to be the foundation stone of everything the partnership will do together in the jumping arena.

We can continue to put the building blocks on the foundation stone as each stage is successfully completed. We are now going to start controlling and exercising the hindquarter power simply by working on the transitions from canter to halt and halt to canter. The asking aids are the same as in the two main transitions, walk to trot and trot to canter but there is a positive variation on the theme because we are coming from a powerful gait, the canter, to a standstill. There is not the obvious follow through of movement like, say, trot to canter. The power of the rider's seat and the willing obedience of the horse are the vital ingredients to the success of this phase just as they will be on the field of competition.

The exercise starts with the horse and rider at a balanced canter. Then on one of the long sides of the schooling arena about halfway along the rider closes his hands while pushing the horse's body through his seat and lower legs up to his resisting hands. The rider will feel the power of the horse's hind legs as they come under him to prepare for the halt and at almost precisely the same time the give of the horse's mouth as he comes to the halt. But instead of opening the hand now – to say: 'Thank you very much, you've done it' – the rider keeps his hands closed with the horse standing for a few seconds. Then down comes the push of the rider's seat aid again backed up by the squeezing of the lower legs but remember the hands are still *closed*. This time the rider will feel the power coming up from the horse's hindquarters, a lightening of the forehand and almost a rocking action as the horse strikes off into the canter. This is a critical moment for the rider, just as take-off is in jumping, for immediately he feels his horse strike off to the canter he must keep

3

2

4

1

(1) Addie has sat well down in the saddle to ask for the transition from trot to canter. There is a little resistance in Rollo's body but he has quickly and willingly obeyed the aids. On the next stride (2) he has softened, come down to the bridle and started to put power into his transition. In the next (3), Rollo has lowered his croup and started to bring his hindlegs well under, and in the final shot (4) we see him taking that magic uphill attitude of his body to stride away in a good canter

up the pressure of his seat aid and lower legs to maintain the power of the canter but open his fingers and release the resistance of his hands. Taking that back to our original dialogue, the rider has simply said: 'The door is open now, so through you go'.

None of this is achieved, of course, in a couple of days but with diligent and patient regular work you will be amazed what measure of *willing* control can be gained over the horse's mind and body in a couple of weeks. And you will be even more pleased by the amount of muscle and power your horse will develop!

We will assume you now have control over balance, rhythm, transitions and the magic key to your horse's mouth. So let's erect the next building block.

HALF-HALT (see pp100-3)

If we forget the actual jumping of the fences for the moment show-jumping is all about asking the horse to lengthen when going for a spread fence and to shorten, come back, for a vertical fence. That is in the simplest terms because later we will discuss how distances set by a course designer test horse and rider on the flat. When we are competing in the show arena we are going to need a horse that will 'come back' to us and 'go away' from us with smoothness, power and, above all, calmness. One of the most important exercises in the groundwork to that discipline is the half-halt. This encourages, once again, submission to the bridle, obedience to the rider's leg and seat aids, balance, calmness and co-ordination between horse and rider. It is a simple exercise requiring no special facilities or even a great deal of room. The long side of the schooling arena can be used or any straight line such as a paddock fence or hedgerow, in fact, you can even do it while out hacking.

We start, as with everything else, at the sitting trot with the horse settled into an even gait. As the horse comes down a straight line the rider closes and resists with his hands, closes his lower legs and pushes with his seat aid, the forward movement of the horse is checked by his closed hands. The horse gives to the resistance and slows his rate of trot. After a few paces, and only a few, say 4–5yd, the rider opens his hands, again applies the leg and seat aid, and the horse lengthens his stride and goes away. So we have said: 'Come back' and we have said: 'Go away' but it is vital to keep contact with the horse's mouth throughout the exercise. Eventually the same exercise is repeated at the canter. The half-halt should be done every day throughout a showjumping horse's career including warming up in the collecting ring. You will be delighted with the results as you gradually feel your horse become smoothly and willingly responsive while your aids (in the riding dialogue, 'come back', 'go away') will become as light and as simple as saying the words to your horse in the ring.

CHANGING REIN

So far we have been basically working on straight lines but modern showjumping courses now include several changes of rein (direction) and course designers are putting even more emphasis on this in jump-off courses against the clock. So 'our' showjumper must now be worked through the changes of rein.

We must first of all understand what we want in showjumping when making a change of rein. This is quite simply, smoothness, balance and no loss of power. All are vital ingredients to a clear round and critical as time-savers in a jump-off. What we do not want is a horse which changes direction leading from his shoulder with his head looking the other way or a horse which comes round a corner with his hindquarters floating away in the other direction. What we do want is a horse that curves his body to the turn or change of direction, moving on a single track and *looking* in the direction he is going.

There are three main exercises we can use to teach the horse to give individual parts of his body to the rider's aids. These are the change of lead at the canter, the turn on the forehand and the shoulder-in haunches-in. The use of these movements in jumping training are not to be confused with their use in the training of the competition dressage horse. The aims of one discipline are not the same as the other. In jumping training we are not looking for a pure classical style and execution, we are not going to be judged on that, but we are looking for an immediate and willing response from the horse to the rider.

Changing the Leading Leg at the Canter

You will know that in the canter the horse leads with the near-fore when cantering to the left and the off-fore when cantering to the right. The hind leg of the same side follows the track of the leading leg. So, for balance, when we change direction in the jumping arena we need the horse to change his lead . . . and not just in front but behind as well! Going disunited into a fence will often mean a rail on the floor or most certainly loss of vital seconds in a jump-off.

We start off at the canter on a figure of eight and as the horse comes across the diagonal of the eight the rider brings him back to the trot and then asks for the new leading leg for the other direction. To ask the horse for the correct lead the rider slightly raises the asking hand to the side of the change of direction and increases the pressure of his opposite lower leg to give the signal to the horse, eg the right lead. The rider's weight in the saddle is inclined to the opposite side of the turn. For example, when asking for the right lead with hands and legs the rider's weight is put on the left seat-bone to keep the turn or change of direction square and balanced. If the horse misunderstands or does not make the change then come

1

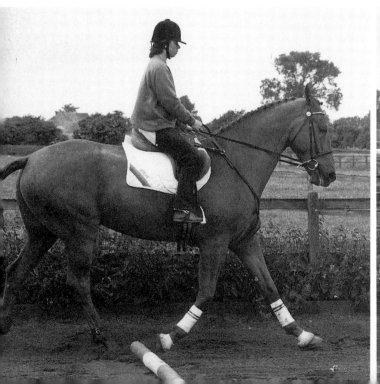

2

The Half-Halt. In this sequence Addie has asked Rollo to shorten his stride (1) but the horse has resisted her closed hands (2 and 3) and then when she asks him to go on through the bridle and lengthen his stride he has given about a 60%

4

5

answer (4). Then on being asked again to come back to the shorter stride his resistance has come through once more (5 and 6)

1

Now they are getting their act together. Rollo has answered all of Addie's aids, seat and hands, holding the short active stride (1) and then bursting away with plenty of power and willingness to the longer stride (2 and 3) before returning nicely to the short, balanced stride once again (4). This is the most important

3

2

exercise in the entire programme of the training of a jumping horse no matter what level he is going to compete at and you can see quite clearly the theory 'No, stay here, the door is closed' and 'Now, the door is open, go on through'

4

back to the trot and ask again on the next diagonal across the figure of eight. Equally if the horse changes in front but not behind, in other words goes disunited, correct it in the same way. If the horse does go disunited, by the way, you will soon know it by the un-comfortable feeling experienced through losing balance and rhythm.

Once that exercise is going well and correctly we change from the figure of eight to two circles. Again the rider brings the horse back to the trot asks for the change of lead and goes on the other circle. Now the period of trot can gradually be shortened until eventually the horse anticipates the change of direction and auto-matically changes his lead. There is nothing wrong with a jumping horse anticipating a movement or change, in fact it's a definite advantage in the competition ring. So the more you can slant your schooling at home to a sort of teach-yourself theme the more effective your horse is going to be as a showjumper. Don't forget, we are going to need that 20 per cent horse on several occasions!

The Turn on the Forehand

The horse is asked to move his hindquarters by crossing one hind leg over the other around his forehand. The horse should pivot or describe a small circle on his foreleg but in jumping training the pivot on the inside foreleg is not essential, a small circle will do, but the horse must step across with the hind legs. When turning to the right the off-fore will be describing a small circle but the horse must not take a step back or forward, that would defeat the object of the exercise. The rider's right leg is drawn back behind the girth; a squeeze is applied on the right rein by the right hand but the horse's head must not actually turn. The rider's left leg is held at the girth to restrain the horse from stepping backwards, and to be ready to ask him to move forwards when the figure is completed. A long schooling stick is helpful when first starting this exercise to back up the rider's asking leg and to teach the horse to give to the aid and move his haunches away.

We can add to this exercise gradually by first asking the horse to walk on briskly after the turn, then to trot on immediately and finally to go straight away into the canter. The reason for doing this is that we need total 'call' on the horse's hindquarters and power from any given position or angle. There is very little practical use in this turn itself but it is a very efficient exercise for discipline and quick response to the rider.

The Shoulder-in Haunches-in

These exercises are designed to supple the horse's body but we get the added bonus from them in showjumping training of practising control over the shoulders and hindquarters of the horse. We start off in shoulder-in quite simply using the corners of the schooling arena. As the horse and rider come through a corner, the rider asks with the left rein as if to continue with a complete circle to, let's say, the left. With the right rein the rider does not allow the horse to describe that circle. The rider's left lower leg is pressed at the girth, to encourage the horse to go forward on a line, and the right leg is squeezing slightly behind the girth to keep the hind legs on the track. The hindquarters must stay on their original track while the horse moves forward with his right shoulder leading the left hip and his left shoulder moving outside his right hip. This asks the horse to bend his body around the pressure of the rider's left leg and to place his hocks well under him. Both actions produce overall suppleness and a powerful stride from the hind legs.

Once again, by exercising the horse's ability to produce impulsion with the minimum effort and strain we will have power at our call in the jumping ring. The exercise must be taken in slow, progressive stages, the rider asking for the movement for only short sequences and, if the rider does not get the right response each time, the horse should be allowed to carry on and complete the circle. Eventually the horse will hold the shoulder-in attitude for the entire length of the exercise area. The exercise, of course, should be worked on both reins.

Haunches-in is an exercise with precisely the same aims, on another theme, as the shoulder-in but this time we are working on the control of the hindquarters. Again the figure should be started on a corner and working from a walk to a trot as soon as possible. This time the rider's left lower leg pushes the hindquarters – as it did in the turn on the forehand – away from the track of the forehand. The rider's left hand is closed (active) and the right hand is open (passive). His lower right leg is kept at the girth to hold the forehand on the original track. The exercise is carried out on both reins.

We now have willing obedience, suppleness, control over power and balance. We know the daily work-out routine in the 'gymnasium' and now it's time for the end-product of all this work . . . the jumping.

CHAPTER 6

Jumping Technique

Now that we have completed our groundwork and brought the horse up to be an educated, responsive and obedient ride we can start on the gymnastic training for the real meat of the training programme . . . jumping.

The early stages of the programme are carried out at the sitting trot only and the direction, left rein and right rein, is changed about every ten to fifteen minutes. The sitting trot gives the rider more feel of what his horse is doing, encourages a better jumping position over an obstacle and for the young horse it encourages him to use his power rather than speed when jumping.

CAVALLETTI WORK

We have two aims in cavalletti work:

1 Efficient control over the horse's strides.
2 Effective muscle-building and supplying of the horse.

I do not use real cavalletti for this work, instead I use coloured poles on the ground and/or slightly raised. After all, it is coloured rails the horse is going to jump in the ring, so the sooner these are used and he gets confident working over them the better.

The trotting poles are laid out on the two long sides of the schooling area so that we have two grids. On one side place three poles on the ground set to simulate short distances about 3ft (90cm) apart. On the other side place three poles to represent the long stride, at about 3ft 6in (1.05m) apart. These distances are not hard-and-fast rules as each horse is just that bit different in the length and rhythm of his trot. If you first let the horse walk down both grids on a loose rein he will show you the space he is going to need to go through the grid on an even stride, for example, he may step over the first rail and then knock the second one or do a little 'shuffle' to correct his stride and so on. The poles on the ground can then be adjusted until the horse walks over them cleanly and within the rhythm of his steps.

It's a good idea to have two poles on the ground next to each other in the centre of the schooling ring so that each session can be started by just letting the horse walk quietly and freely over each one . . . walking over one then back over the other. Then let him have a free trot over them. This will show the horse what the morning's work is going to be all about and both he and the rider will loosen up their muscles and joints ready for the grids.

The rider's job, at this stage, is to guide the horse down the middle of each grid regulating the pace, slow for the short-striding grid and a longer, more powerful rhythm for the long grid. The rider will be using all his aids: hands, legs and seat-bones to keep impulsion and regularity in the horse's gait. I like to see all this work done with as free a rein as possible so that the horse is encouraged to use his head and neck for balance as he negotiates each grid. If the horse rushes at the grids or resists the rider's aids then he can be taken back to walking and trotting over the single rails in the centre until he is settled and listening to his rider. Always try and find some way of letting the horse see how you want him to go. He will soon learn what is being asked of him and how he is expected to carry it out.

For our purposes we will assume that everything is going nice and smoothly and before very long the horse will start flexing his joints and suspending his steps to negotiate each grid cleanly. The rider will feel this through an elevated rocking rhythm down the grids. Once this stage has been reached our horse is on the way to becoming some sort of a showjumper having learned to control each step with accuracy and power.

As soon as the horse starts to show us this bounce, and the rider demonstrates the degree of control he has over the rhythm, the trotting poles can be raised slightly to flex the horse's joints more and really start to ask just that little bit more of his accuracy. We do this by simply resting one end of the pole on the barrier of the schooling ring. But any system, such as placing bricks or rubber tyres under the ends of the poles, will do the job just as well. Now this time we vary the programme by changing from just simply trotting around the arena to starting from a circle in the centre of the ring and adding in the half-halt exercise on the short side of the arena before going to the second grid of poles. What we are doing is introducing two vital factors, which we worked on in our dressage schooling, that we are going to need when we start jumping our first fences.

Working over a rail-grid on the ground. Addie just lets Rollo help himself down a grid of four rails at the walk. She has left his head and neck free and we can see how Rollo is looking down to measure his footfalls between the rails. He is calm and relaxed about the whole thing and we have the distances right between the rails for his length of stride

Addie has now brought Rollo under full control and asked him to trot down the grid. Look at the wonderful flexion of the joints he is giving us and the evenness of his stride, while he still remains calm and willing. These grids are the 'wall-bars' of jumping training: they not only encourage horse and rider to know exactly where each footfall is, but they also build muscle and balance in both

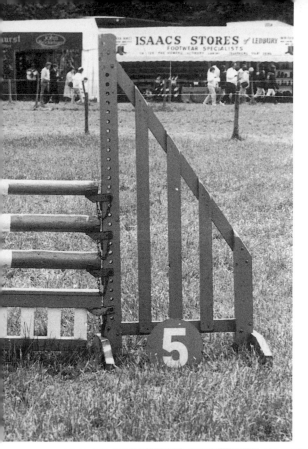

Show fences are designed basically on two forms, the vertical (1) and the spread (2)

By starting from a circle, still at the sitting trot, we can ask the horse to make different approaches to the grids. For example, if we start coming out of a small circle we will be asking for a short-angled approach to the first grid and if we start coming out of a large circle we will be asking for a long approach. By bringing in the half-halt after going down the first grid we are asking the horse to come back to us and then to go away again just as we would if we were going from one fence to another on a showjumping course. So you see we can use these gymnastic sessions in direct relation to the future – showjumping. We are also getting the bonus of using that little ingredient we have mentioned several times so far . . . variety.

Within a few days the horse will be elevating and regulating his steps with bounce and accuracy. More simply, our potential jumper knows where he is putting his feet and how to use his power. A good jumping technique is based upon sound knowledge of rhythm and timing and that applies to both the horse and the rider. So now we have brought rhythm and timing into the horse's vocabulary we can begin to work on the rider as well.

Until now the rider has done nothing more than he would have done on any intermediate or advanced equitation course. Now that the jumping of obstacles is about to come into our training programme the rider, too, must work on technique, balance and timing. This is a good moment to study the position of the rider whilst jumping.

THE APPROACH

The most important stage of jumping for the rider is the approach to a fence, ie presenting the horse to a fence. It is at this phase that the horse judges his jump and it is now that the rider gives the horse the most assistance. Try to remember all the time that it is the horse which does the actual jumping not the rider! Without a good approach an accurate jump cannot be achieved although many seem to carry on jumping fences in spite of their riders.

A bad approach or poor, mistimed presentation will put the horse at a disadvantage in relation to the fences. An inactive approach, for example, will ask too much of the horse's body when the time comes for him to power himself into the air. An over-active approach will encourage the horse to flatten over a fence and he will, quite rightly, become careless. As he presents his horse to a fence the rider sits slightly more forward than for riding on the flat. He concentrates on keeping his horse straight and going for the centre of the fence. The rider's weight is supported by the flexibility of his ankles, his lower leg is used in a squeezing action in rhythm with his seat-aid to drive the horse up to the fence.

Presentation is the rider's most important participation with the horse in jumping. Addie has brought Rollo off a circle and presented him nice and straight for a small cross-rails practice fence (1). The horse is looking to the fence and they meet it on a nice stride (2) and just 'pop' over it (3)

Here the rider has presented the horse too deep for a vertical (1) and the horse is having to put tremendous pressure on his hocks to come up and try to find room for his jump. In the next shot (2) we see he has found room and the rider has given him the freedom of his head and neck, but in the next frame (3) we can see that the horse has reached the highest point of his jump after the top rail, and he is going to have to be quick and clever in order to tip his hind end and avoid having the rail off with a hindleg or foot

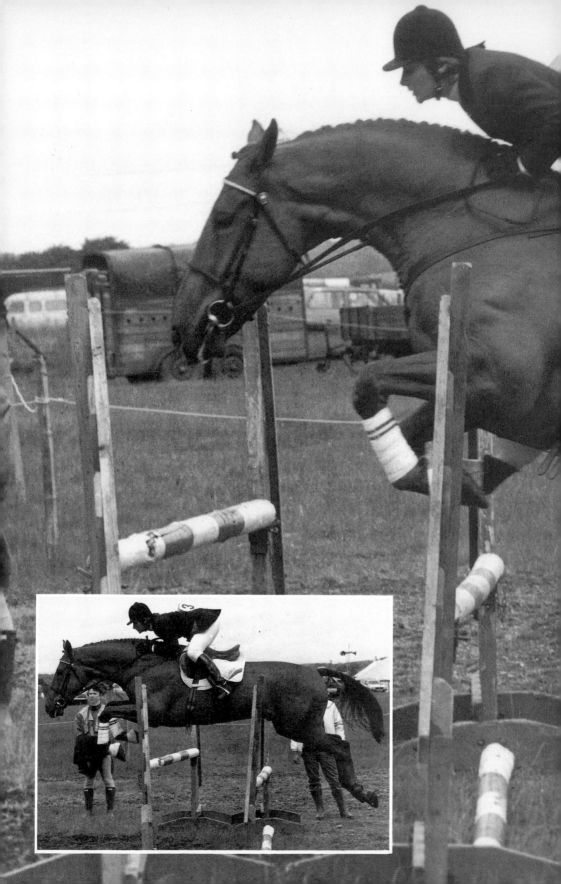

This time horse and rider have met this spread just about right. The horse has taken off at almost a half-stride away from the front rail but the rider has got ahead of the horse, leaving her pivoting on her knees at the highest point of the jump (inset)

Addie demonstrates how the rider's back 'collapses' over the highest point of the horse's jump

Throughout the approach the rider concentrates on controlling pace and direction but also encourages the horse to make the approach calmly. Let the fence come to you instead of chasing towards it. On nearing the fence the rider sits well down into the saddle, inclining the upper body forward and using his seat, in rhythm with the horse's stride, and his leg-pressure to ask the horse to make his jump.

THE TAKE-OFF

As the horse rises into the air the rider's hands follow the line of the horse's neck with the fingers open. His upper body comes forward and down – in a jack-knife action – while his seat comes out of the saddle (but not into the air!) thereby taking the weight off the horse's back and hindquarters (the area from which the horse is getting his lift). The rider's fingers open completely to allow the horse the freedom of his head and neck to make his 'bridge' over the fence. For support, the rider's heels are well down, the stirrup leathers are still in a vertical plane while his upper body has moved further forward but down close to the horse. The rider's weight is cushioned by his thighs, ankles and heels. Although giving freedom to the horse's head and neck in flight the rider must maintain a light contact with the horse's mouth through the reins. Try not to fall into the trap of gripping with your knees and pivoting on the horse's back in the air.

The Flight

During the actual flight and landing, the most thrilling part of jumping, the rider is very much a passenger and little is demanded of him except to keep his forward position, the contact of the lower legs and to take his weight on his ankles and thighs.

Two completely different styles but both very effective and highly successful. First, Austria's former Volvo World Cup Champion, Hugo Simon, a very positive and attacking competitor. Hugo may not be the most classical stylist in the game but just look at the freedom he gives his horse in the air! On the right David Broome, the master himself, gives us a perfect demonstration of the rider's back 'collapsing' over a fence and his hands following the trajectory of his horse. Study particularly David's lovely open, sensitive hands. It's the horse that does the jumping, not the rider, and at this point of his jump this horse is getting no interference from 'upstairs'!

As the horse prepares to land, the rider lowers her seat back into the saddle to be ready for the first non-jumping stride after the fence

LANDING

As the horse begins to land the rider must slowly return his seat into the saddle but keep his upper body inclined forward. A good guide line is to try to keep a line from the horse's mouth through the rider's hands to the elbow throughout the bascule of the jump.

RECOVERY OR NEXT APPROACH

The last stage in jumping is the recovery or next approach. This sounds very simple but many riders tend to forget there are more fences to come on a showjumping course – one good jump is not enough.

The rider sights his next fence, sits down in the saddle, brings his upper body back again to the near-upright and prepares his horse again for the next approach and take-off.

The rider's jumping technique may sound simple and straight-forward but there is a little bit more to it than just sitting correctly over a fence. To gain that little bit extra that all jumping riders must have, try to understand and perfect the approach and the presentation to the fence.

STRIDE

You have probably heard the expression, 'seeing a stride', and this is what we are going to discuss now before returning to the training of our jumping horse. Without a sense of seeing a stride a jumping rider cannot achieve a good presentation of his horse to each show fence (or any other obstacle for that matter).

We have already established that the horse does not get over a fence by some magic spring in his hind legs. What he does do is 'lift' his body into the air by means of several action points and his forward movement. These action points operate in approximately the following sequence: the length of the stride of the hind legs (these give the launching power to the horse's body, so his ability to jump fences cleanly depends on how active the horse is in his hind legs); how strong he is in his thigh and how far he can place his hocks under his body on the final strides to the take-off. As the horse approaches his point of take-off he will lean his weight back on his hindquarters and legs thus tightening his forehand. With the power-push of the hind legs, the forehand, particularly the shoulder, will be pushed forward and into the air with the forelegs folding up. The neck comes into play and extends to act as a balancing pole as the forehand becomes suspended and the horse's body begins to form a 'bridge' over the fence. This continues throughout flight but it is the actual launching, as it were, that concerns us at the moment.

A horse measures his fence from the bottom up and a rough guide – which can vary quite a lot with the type of horse and the length of his stride – to the take-off point is one and a half times the height of the fence. For example, for a 3ft (90cm) fence the take-off point would be somewhere between 3ft 6in to 4ft 6in (1.05m to 1.37m) in front of the fence. On seeing where he is going to take off the horse will slightly lower his head to see his stride to make the distance for that take-off. The rider must measure the distance with his eye in the same way. This is where the rider's intelligence and instinct come into play as he must have a natural feeling for rhythm and distance if he and his jumper are to arrive at the right place (and the same place) at the right time.

For some jumping riders these abilities are instinctive but they can be learned and perfected through some simple progressive exercises. We have used the raised trotting rails or cavalletti in our basic gymnastic work with the horse but now we are going to use them to work on the rider to perfect his sense of stride and distance.

Stride Exercises

Place on either side of the schooling arena a coloured pole raised to about 8in to 10in (20cm to 25cm). The rider walks his horse around the schooling arena leaving the horse's head absolutely free. While doing this he encourages the horse to walk with as much activity as possible. He must do nothing more than this as the horse is going to teach him rhythm and distance. As the horse approaches the rail he will look slightly down as he measures the distance the rail is away from within the rhythm of his walk. The rider will feel this and he will feel whether the stride of the walk is even to meet the rail. If the horse's stride is even he will walk over the rail without changing the rhythm of that stride. Then as he comes round to the other side he will see the second pole and react in the same way. If the horse has been walking on well he will not have made any change in his stride when walking over the poles. The rider, remember, is leaving the horse's head free and controlling only the activity of the forward movement.

127

Practising strides. Here we have two stride rails on the ground set at one non-jumping stride from a very simple cross-rails. Rollo has remembered his homework (1 and 2) and got in a good non-jumping stride in front of the fence

(3) but although Addie has collapsed her back well she has not followed through with her hands, and has moved her body weight to one side (4). In the competition arena that would have meant a rail down – four faults!

Using only one rail to define the one non-jumping stride before take-off, but this time to a small spread fence (1). Rollo has come in nice and active (2), gone for his non-jumping stride, drawn his hocks well under him for take-off (3) and started a high trajectory. But again Addie has not followed through with her

1

weight and hands, which has left the horse with no option but to flatten his trajectory (4). We can see in the landing shot (5) just how far behind the forward movement the rider was from take-off

4

3

Here we see a much better picture of power and accuracy now coming into technique. But we still have the problem of the rider not following through and coming back down on the saddle too early before landing. This shift of weight

1

against the forward movement interferes with the horse's tip of his body over a fence, and that in turn leads to inaccurate jumping

4   3

Now we start to build on that situation by adding another rail to each side of the schooling arena. The distance between these pairs will be judged similarly to the way we laid out the grid for our jumping horse on average about 3ft to 3ft 6in (90cm to 1.05m) apart. Again the rider is asked to walk round the school leaving his horse's head completely free and encouraging an active walk. Once more, the horse will look slightly down as he approaches the rails but this time he will increase the activity of his limbs to cope with the two poles. In jumping, even in its simplest form, activity must not be confused with pace; pace is the last thing we want at this stage.

The rider will feel this increase in activity so the horse has now started to show the rider when his strides are right for walking over the rails cleanly. The value of this simple, but important, exercise is based on just one fact which is that most horses are creatures of natural grace. They do not like knocking their toes or joints on poles or cavalletti, neither do they enjoy stumbling over things so they correct their momentum and balance to avoid them.

The rider sitting on the horse's back doing almost nothing is given a demonstration of how the horse arrives at the poles so that he can walk evenly over them without touching them. After some fifteen to twenty minutes of this exercise the rider will find that he too is beginning to measure his distances from the poles and is sensing the rhythm which will allow them both (horse and rider) an even passage over and between the two pairs of poles. Once this stage has been reached a third pole or cavalletti is placed with the two pairs and the rider asked, once again, to just sit there and listen.

The process can now be taken to the next step. Replace the third pole on each side of the arena with a small jump. On one side of the schooling arena make this a small vertical jump and on the other side a narrow spread. Under both of them place a bar on the ground to form a baseline. Horse and rider are now asked to come into a steady sitting trot but the rider must still leave the horse the freedom of his head and neck. All we want the rider to do is to concentrate on the suppleness of his waist and go with the horse.

Conditions are now getting nearer to a jumping situation. Horse and rider know where the poles are and the horse has shown the rider what stride and how much activity he needs to negotiate

This is more the shape and form we are aiming at. The rider has gone with the trajectory and, although not completely following through with her hands, she is helping the horse to make his 'shape' over the fence

A simple double set up with one long non-jumping stride, and on a turn from the spread in the background

Rollo gets in one nice, even, long non-jumping stride inside and looks for his take-off spot for the second element

I often use two rails leaning on practice fences and slanted towards the centre. These encourage a young horse (or rider) to go for the middle of the fence, with the added bonus that they can make even the simplest of fences look more solid and inviting

them. But now at the trot and with a small jump, say 2ft 6in to 2ft 9in (75cm to 85cm) included, the horse will need more activity and will naturally put more thought into the rhythm of his stride. For the small upright the rider will feel his horse looking for a spot to take off from and this spot will be closer to the fence than that for the small spread. He will also notice or feel that the horse lowers his head slightly on approaching the jump and extends his neck after passing the last pole on the ground. Because the horse is left to make his own decisions and the object of the exercise is for the rider to learn by feel and observation, there will be occasions when the horse will make corrections to his balance and movement. For instance, he may just slightly check his stride when approaching the first ground pole or increase his activity (impulsion) before coming to the two other poles and small jump.

On another occasion he may mistime his movement over the poles on the ground and correct it by taking a short stride just before take-off over the jump, by taking one longer stride, by getting very close to the jump or by missing a stride completely and taking off further back from the obstacle. The rider will see and feel all these conditions. Before very long the rider, through feel, will start to anticipate when and where the horse is going to change his stride, rhythm and activity. In other words he will begin to *see* a stride!

All these exercises have been carried out at the sitting trot but there will be times when the horse will break into a canter, perhaps on the approach to the jump or on landing after it, but this really doesn't matter too much and the rider can just encourage the horse to return to a calm trot. When it does happen it is usually because the horse is trying too hard to please.

CHAPTER 7

Practice Makes Perfect

All that is needed now is practice and polishing of technique before the moment of truth – the first public outing. Practice, they say, makes perfect and no matter how threadbare that may sound it is no less than the *only* way to success. Some may and can take short-cuts to the top but they have a habit of slipping down to the second division by the shortest of all routes. The really top-notch performer comes from the practical and real school of rehearse, rehearse and rehearse again. This is particularly true of competitive showjumping whether it be in Great Britain, France, Australia or the United States of America. It is also true now of the USSR, East Germany, Poland and Hungary. To be successful in showjumping today, whether in junior, senior, novice or open divisions, your horse or pony must be totally responsive and accurate and your riding must be completely effective all the way from the warming-up ring to crossing the finishing line.

It is often in this practice phase that many trainers and riders are tempted to disregard a graduated training programme by trying to take on more than they have the confidence to tackle. Any impetuosity at this stage can destroy weeks of careful training so make haste slowly. Take one step at a time and do not move on to the next stage until you feel absolutely confident that you know what you are doing and that the horse knows what he is doing. If you have set a timetable for the training programme and the horse falls behind, then more often than not it is the schedule and not the horse that is in need of revision. For this finishing-off stage we move from the grids and single fences to the jumping lane, or chute, and a full practice course.

THE JUMPING LANE

The jumping lane encourages suppleness and quick reflexes in both the horse and the rider. These are principles we have touched on before but this time they will be directly related to the job of jumping fences as opposed to preparation on the flat. Once the horse has entered the chute the rider can concentrate and relax, simply riding forward, thinking about the presentation to each fence and maintaining a good rhythm as the fences come along in a regulated sequence. Once the horse can come down the chute at a steady regular canter 'popping' over low oxers double cross-rails and a small gate calmly and cleanly, then he is ready to make the transition to a laid-out course of show fences.

THE PRACTICE COURSE

Many horses find the transition from jumping straight lines of fences to a laid-out course with changes of direction in a wide open space an invitation to quicken their pace or get excited about their jumping. To alleviate this temptation the practice course should first be set very low, and the horse trotted over the first fence then asked to canter over the second and so on. But if he shows signs of quickening too much, then trot over the first two fences and canter to the third and so on.

At this stage I like to present the horse (and I have in mind here a young novice jumper) to the first fence then on landing, circle, say to the right, then come round and jump the second fence, then circle to the left, and so on. I find this system encourages the young horse (and a novice rider) to collect himself quickly on landing and gives the rider a better chance of making a good presentation to each fence. I even use this circling/jumping/circling exercise in double and treble combinations. If the horse has been brought through his groundwork and obedience training correctly, this circling exercise will not tempt him to run out or duck out at his fences. On the contrary, I find it makes the horse more responsive and supple. This work should be continued for at least a week, gradually decreasing the size of the circles to get the horse to bend cleanly and give his mouth to the bridle before and after each fence. After about ten days the horse will negotiate a small course of show fences smoothly, rhythmically and, most of the time cleanly.

I mentioned at the beginning of this chapter that many riders, and some coaches, are tempted to disregard a graduated training programme by trying to take on more than they have the confidence to tackle. It is at this stage that the temptation to assume the horse is a jumper often raises its ugly head. It happens to all of us at some time in our riding careers or lives.

Jumping Lane or Chute

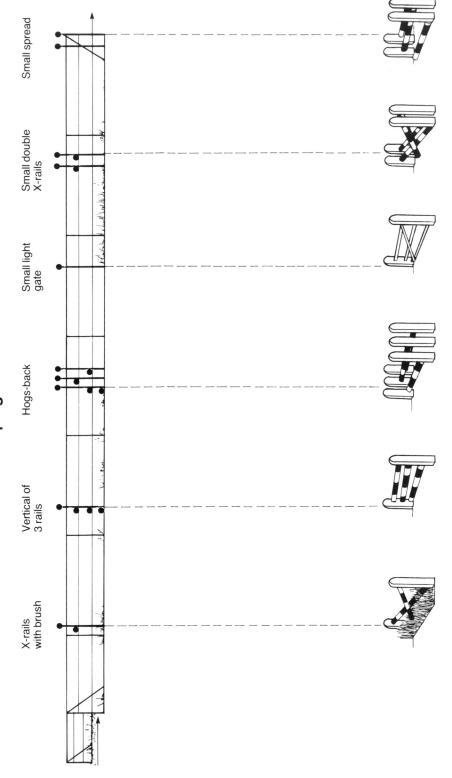

X-rails
with brush

Vertical of
3 rails

Hogs-back

Small light
gate

Small double
X-rails

Small spread

Suggested layout for a "Schooling" course

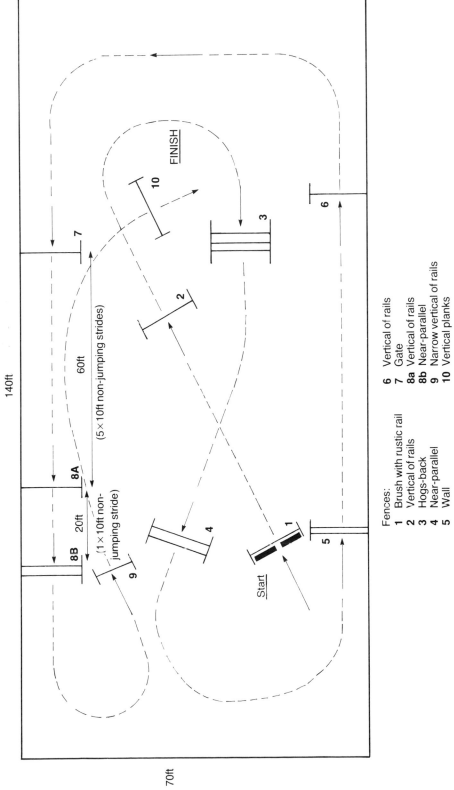

Fences:
1 Brush with rustic rail
2 Vertical of rails
3 Hogs-back
4 Near-parallel
5 Wall
6 Vertical of rails
7 Gate
8a Vertical of rails
8b Near-parallel
9 Narrow vertical of rails
10 Vertical planks

The truth is, we have so far followed a slow graduated programme. We have not, or hope we have not, asked anything complicated of our horse. We have tried to help him through any problems by lowering fences. We have not overpaced the horse at any time. The whole basis of a graduated programme is to build the confidence of the horse in his jumping and, as the programme moves on to more testing training, it is now that we must keep the horse's confidence and above all his trust in whatever the rider asks of him.

If there is a secret to producing a showjumper it is this trust which must exist between horse and rider and between horse, rider and coach. The same is true, of course, of all forms of equitation. The object of showjumping is to get over, preferably without touching, a series of artificial obstacles. Showjumping, as an equestrian sport, is unique in that horse and rider are asked to perform within the confines of an arena. In racing, the most natural sport we use the horse for, we take advantage of his herd instinct. In dressage, as a competition event as against training, we are taking advantage of the natural airs and graces shown by the horse, particularly a colt or stallion, when out in the paddock or in the wild. The same is true of cross-country riding which through its origins in the hunting field is perhaps the oldest of all horse sports. Horse and rider are to a certain extent still in their natural environment, the wide open spaces of the great outdoors and competing at speed.

In showjumping there are none of these natural stimulants. The fences are man-made. There is no herd from which to draw security. Horse and rider are out in the ring on their own. The 'natural' school of riding works on the principle that the horse can be educated to think for himself, and, with the minimum interference from the rider, be trained to jump his fences willingly and fluently. The origins of this theory go back many years. The man who brought the horse off the treadmill of severe bridles and long spurs was Captain Federico Caprilli (1868–1907), the creator of what his followers were to call the 'forward seat'.

Caprilli was an Italian Cavalry Officer and an instructor at the Cavalry School, Pinerolo, in 1904. As a young lieutenant serving in a small garrison in southern Italy, the fun-loving Federico worked out a new *sistema* that was to be sheer genius in its simplicity. It was to become known as the Italian seat, the forward impulse, the forward seat and now more generally as the natural school. It took horsemanship away from the firm traditions of severe bits, the violent jerking of the horse's head, the over-use of sharp spurs and the rider's dependence on the reins. Domination was replaced by education.

Although frowned on at first it was not long before he and his pupils were doing well in competition. Eventually the system spread all over the world with many old and established military schools completely rewriting their manuals. The principle of Caprilli's system (Principi di Equitazione di Campagna, 1901) was that the rider should interfere with his horse as little as possible and that the horse should go with the freedom and natural balance of a riderless horse. To achieve this the horse has to be 'educated' to the best of his ability and once at that state to be left alone as much as possible. In other words, the horseman encourages the horse to learn his job by using whatever in-born qualities he has; trains him to retain this knowledge and act upon it; to willingly accept the rider and his signals as a partner in the operation and not as a slave.

Up to this time riders had adopted the classical seat: straight legs, stiff backs and fixed hands. But now the position in the saddle changed dramatically, it came forward in all senses of the word. The rider was positioned in the middle of the saddle, his back became more supple and relaxed, the stirrup leathers were shorter to enable the rider to follow the natural free forward movement of the horse. Over-exaggerated collection was cancelled out with a freer rein hand, allowing the horse to come to a natural state of collection and flexion. But more important still, the horse was encouraged to use his head and neck, his natural balancing pole, for greater efficiency and fluency of performance.

Caprilli's method is now accepted as the basis for all modern techniques particularly in the competition field of showjumping. In training, if we are to take it seriously at all, one is often talking about the ideal world and looking, quite rightly, for perfection. But the world is often not ideal and the nearest we can get to perfection is the best that we can do with the best our horse is capable of giving. There comes a time of honest analysis in any programme. Are we ready to go onto the next stage? Have we completed this phase of the programme correctly? How do we judge these things? The simple answer to all three questions is the horse tells us!

During each stage we have covered your horse will be telling you something. You will see him physically improve. He will be more mentally alert but above all he will be more confident. It is this last factor which is the critical one . . . confidence. The rider can judge this through 'feel' in other words communication. Many riders spend too much time thinking about themselves. How do I look? Have I got my heels down? Am I doing this or should I be doing that? Better to turn these questions around the other way. How does my horse look? Is he coming back to me and going away from me smoothly? Does he feel confident in his work?

Gifted riders are born with an instinctive sense of feel. But riding is one of those rare sports in which those who are not so gifted can still get a lot of fun and satisfaction. One can say the same about horses. Not every horse is going to be a world-class Grand Prix jumper but most of them are capable of winning a few rosettes and of giving their riders considerable enjoyment.

Throughout each schooling session and each step of your training programme concentrate all the time on feeling how your horse is going. Ask yourself: Is he balanced? Are his paces smooth and regulated? Is he concentrating? Is he listening to me? And, above all, is he giving me a better ride at each schooling session? Horses have many ways of 'talking' to us and showing us that they are not happy in their work. Their paces become irregular and sloppy. They become passive and less active. They get careless over trotting poles or in their jumping. There are no hard-and-fast rules in jumping training or jumping riding. The rider, and hopefully the trainer, must concentrate on interpreting feel. It is through this, and only this, that the horse will give *you* the green light for go or the red light for stop.

If during and after each session working over your practice fences your horse has given you the feel of smoothness and balance in his paces and of going willingly with obedient confidence then he is ready to go on to the next stage. If he has given you quite the opposite feel then take him back to working on the flat for a while. That 20 per cent horse which we have mentioned several times can also be turned around to 20 per cent rider. A book, training film or coach can help and guide you but what is more important they can get you thinking about your subject and concentrating on improving. That's the 20 per cent rider element, the grey area where nobody else can go. You are sitting on the horse. You will get the feel of how he is going and progressing and very often this comes down to quite simply a comfortable or an uncomfortable ride. It is rather like the racehorse trainer's technique. After a race, win or lose, he will ask his jockey, how did my horse run? And nine times out of ten he will base his future plans for that horse on his jockey's report.

Jumping training is not all that different. You can discuss with your coach, when you are working with him or her, how the training session felt and he or she can compare that to how it looked from the ground. Out of that will come the decisions and plans for the next stage.

AIMS OF USING PRACTICE FENCES

We can start bringing it all together; first, by summing up the aims and objects of working over practice fences:

1 The main object of the exercise is to improve technique and performance and this must be seen to be done. If it is not, then somebody is not really working, or thinking, and it is back to the drawing board!
2 The course should be as varied as possible with the fences 'dressed' with any interesting material you can lay your hands on like flower boxes, small trees, baseboards or cut birch.
3 The course should be determined beforehand and the rider made to walk the course so that he can get into the habit of thinking and talking through approaches and distances.
4 The dimensions of the fences should be easy to start off with progressing to 3ft 6in (1.05m) or 3ft 9in (1.15m) with spreads of about 3ft 6in (1.05m).
5 If there are any problems, then take the horse back to the jumping lane to regain his confidence.
6 Variety, remember, is the spice of life, so change the layout of the course from time to time.
7 Always finish a schooling session on a good note. If things have gone well and the horse has jumped a good practice round then finish on that. If things have not gone too well, then lower the fences and trot the horse over three or four and finish on that.
8 To maintain continuity, always have someone with you during practice sessions, not necessarily a professional coach, but a person who is involved who can spot faults and help you and the horse to better your performance. That same person can rebuild fences or replace fallen rails . . . saving you a great deal of time and frustration!
9 Always be in search of knowledge and advice, seek out and listen to constructive comments on your horse's and your own performance from experienced horse people. Ask them to come down to watch you on a practice session one morning. Think about

Suggested layout for practising "Jump-off" courses

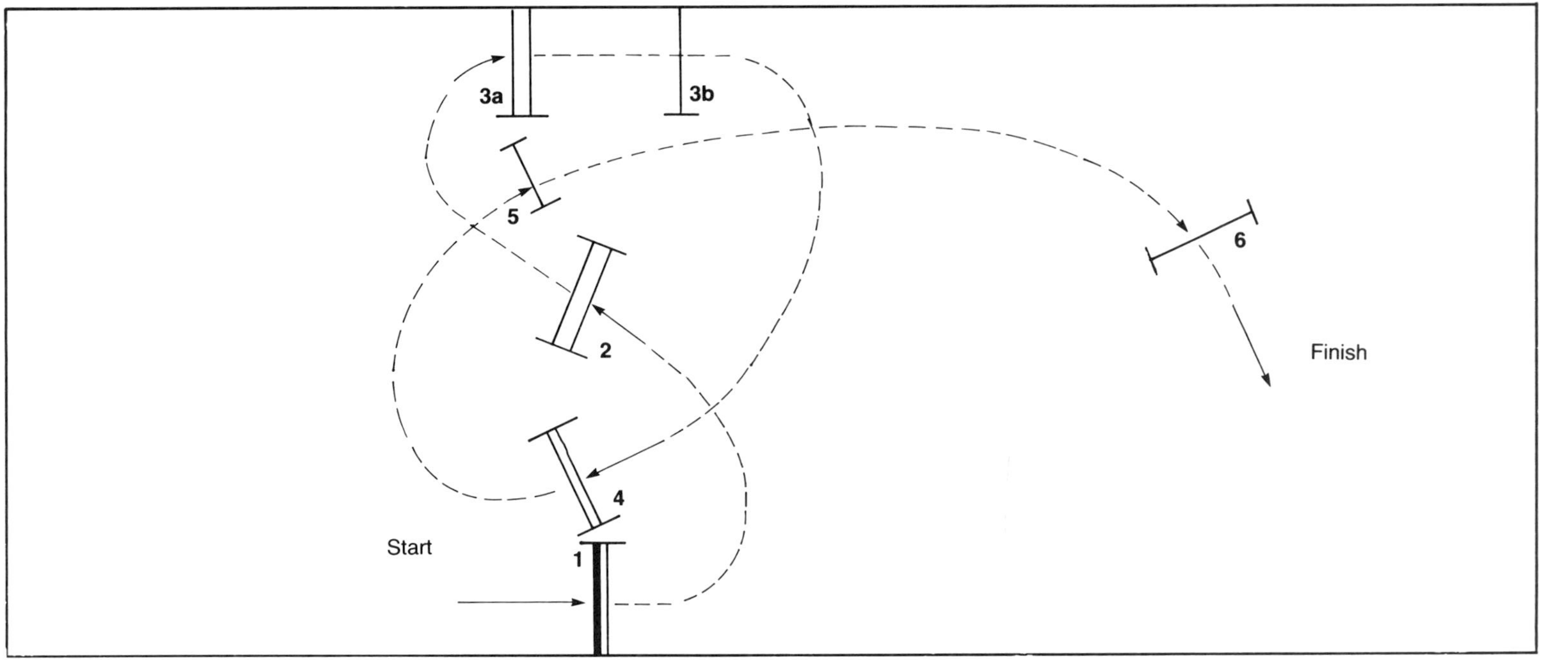

Start

Finish

Fences:

1 Brush with rustic rail
2 Near-parallel
3a Near-parallel
3b Vertical

4 Wall
5 Narrow vertical
6 Planks

taking some private lessons at this stage or join a showjumping clinic. Most national federations, riding clubs and training centres organise teach-ins or clinics, often under very well-known trainers. Top international riders, amateur and professional, profit from the observant attention of coaches as a part of the game, so why not you and your jumper?

Teach-ins and clinics can be of great value and help to the owner/rider but they do have the drawback of being very intensive for three or four days or the duration of the clinic but when the rider gets his horse back home that intensity tends to drop. Regular coaching tends to mean continuity. There are many ways that the private owner can get regular coaching but one of the most effective is to join a riding club. There is no better incentive for improvement than working with other people who have the same aims and ambitions as yourself. The majority of riding clubs in Britain are affiliated to the British Horse Society and its riding club office at Stoneleigh, Warwickshire, will always advise members and potential members.

Exercises
Now that the horse is jumping a simple, but not all that small, course of show fences the time has come for the final stages of the training programme. We can now test the horse with distances and approaches, as the course designer will do when horse and rider get into real competition. We can do this by setting an exercise using three fences and by playing with the double and treble combinations. This is a sort of 'three finger' exercise for jumping riding. We set three individual fences, a vertical, a parallel and an oxer, to form a triangle. This layout gives horse and rider a design on which they practise angled approaches, distances and optional approaches. By now we should be able to accurately judge the stride of our novice jumper so we can set the triangle to give, say, a four to five stride even distance on the angle between fence 1 and/or fences 2 and 3.

First, the horse and rider settle into a nice active and rhythmic canter on a circle just in front of the centre of fence 1. When the rider feels the horse is 'listening' to him he brings the horse in to jump fence 1. On landing he canters on down the schooling arena and turns on his right rein to jump fence 2, but this time on landing he comes round on his right rein and goes for fence 3. From fence 3 horse and rider turn on the right rein to jump fence 1 again and re-

149

Three-fence exercise

Showing one track that can be
taken, but of course there can
and should be several variations.
The distances will depend on the
length of the horse's stride.

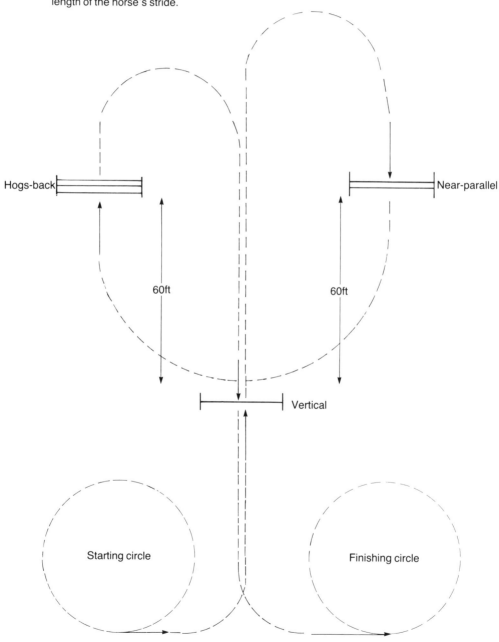

Hogs-back

Near-parallel

60ft

60ft

Vertical

Starting circle

Finishing circle

150

turn to the circle at the canter. This routine can be varied between working on the left rein and working on the right.

We can start to make this exercise more complicated, still only working with three fences. This time horse and rider jump fence 1 at an angle – still approaching from a circle – then they must regulate their stride by counting one, two, three, four and five, for example, and go for fence 2 on an angle. From fence 2 they make a turn-back to jump fence 1 in the opposite direction and then turn back to the third fence. The variations that can be achieved on this simple triangle design are almost endless, working on angled approaches, angled jumps and judging even distances.

Doubles and Trebles

In double and treble combinations a course designer sets his distances between each element to suit the average stride of a horse but he can also use this to test his competitors on the flat. Say, for example, he accepts 10ft (3m) as the average stride then he will allow about 5ft (1.5m) for landing from the first element, a 10ft (3m) non-jumping stride, and 5ft (1.5m) for take-off at the second element. That would be a distance of one even non-jumping stride inside a double combination. He can then play with this by making the distance inside the combination long through allowing a 12ft (3.65m) non-jumping stride or short by allowing, say, an 8ft (2.5m) non-jumping stride. We must build and jump similar variations at home.

These distances can be made progressively more difficult according to the type of fences we use for each element of the combination. It is easier for the rider to regulate the horse's stride if he is going into a vertical fence then a spread fence in a long-distance double combination, and going into a spread fence then a vertical fence in the short-distance double combination. In treble combinations a vertical with a long distance to a spread, followed by a true distance to a spread, *or* a spread then a long one-stride distance to a spread, followed by a true two-stride distance to a spread, are the best distances for a novice jumping horse.

Water Jumps

Water jumps or ditches are very much part of most showjumping courses now and the basis of the technique of jumping water or ditches is to see a horse treat them like a spread fence. I place small water troughs under a fence as early as possible on any horse's

Setting "distance" problems

(from right to left)

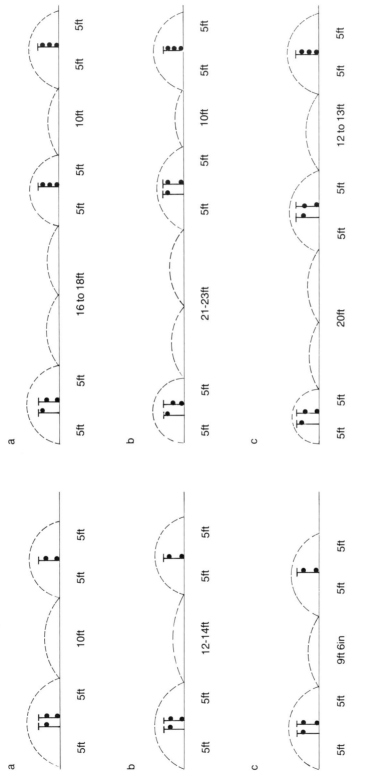

In double combinations:
a) Set at one even non-jumping stride
b) Set at one "long" non-jumping stride
c) Set at one "short" non-jumping stride

In treble combinations:
a) Set at one even non-jumping stride from 1st element to 2nd then two "short" strides to 3rd element
b) Set at one even stride to 2nd element then two "long" strides to 3rd element
c) Set at one "long" stride to 2nd element then two even strides to 3rd element

Basis: 10-12ft stride of horse at about 16.1hh.

training programme. Once a horse has got used to these in his everyday work, ditches, either with water in them or dry, do not seem to present any problems at all. Jumping water is an entirely different subject altogether.

Start off by placing a set of sloping rails from the front of the water to about the centre. As the horse's technique improves, the top rail can be taken away, and so on, until the horse is jumping plain water with confidence and accuracy.

Schooling over water on lunge and under saddle

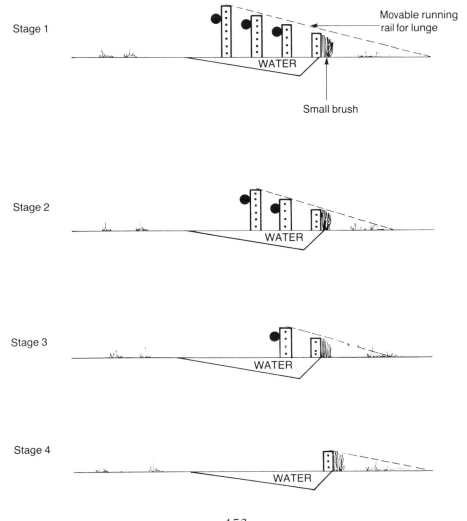

Problems

Our jumper is now well on his way, but what about the problems? Problems are as much a part of the showjumping game as they are of any other sport. So let us take a look at some of the more common problems which can arise, in the hope that this will help you eradicate them at the earliest stage before they become a crisis or major drama.

Rushing

The horse that rushes or gets over-excited about jumping schooling, is usually telling us he is not confident of his jumping ability. The best method to encourage him to be calmer about his jumping is to keep the trotting poles in front of his schooling fences until he does go in and jumps calmly. If he still continues to rush then put him on the lunge rein for a while and let him 'pop' a few fences with two trotting poles in front and two on the landing side. This gives him much more to think about and keeps his mind off worrying about the obstacle itself.

Refusing

This is a delicate question, what to do about the horse that puts in a stop? For some riders he is the worst kind but is he? I would rather have an intelligent horse that will stop at a fence, in effect saying: 'Oh, no! This one's a bit too much for me!' and then come round the second time, get it right and jump it cleanly than the not-so-intelligent horse, but perhaps too brave, who will carry on regardless, crash through the fence and possibly injure himself and his rider. In a competition the winners are the horse and rider that will meet a problem at a fence, live with it, pull themselves together, cock their ears, stick out their little jaws, and go on to the next one as if nothing had happened. But at that level we are concerned with the experienced and confident competitors. At the moment we are thinking of the inexperienced and not so confident. True bravery can only come from confidence and skill and without those two factors bravery can be foolhardy.

If a horse stops at a fence, look for the reasons:

- Was his approach correct?
- Did the rider present the horse to the fence correctly?
- Is the fence too big for the horse at this stage of development?
- Is the rider nervous of jumping?

Once these factors are analysed, lower the fence and come round to it again. If all goes well gradually bring the fence back to its original dimensions. If the horse is an habitual stopper then the horrible truth must be faced, he is not going to make a showjumper. In that situation find something else for him to do because often a horse that cannot adapt to jumping show fences will go and jump cross-country fences at the faster pace with absolute willingness and success.

Running-Out

Once again, this is a sign of lack of confidence, or an intense dislike of jumping although it can often be just plain cheekiness when the horse feels he can take advantage of his rider. Two rails placed either side of each fence resting on the wings will usually solve this problem. If this fails then once more one must face the fact that this particular horse is never going to make a showjumper. If a horse really dislikes jumping it is no use forcing him. The horse will become frightened and develop into a dangerous ride for somebody. Many of the problems met in jumping training are often caused by ourselves through lack of thought and care. So let's now look at some of the more common areas where we often make problems for ourselves and our horses.

Tack and Bitting

Often a rider or trainer will find a horse jumps willingly enough but is inclined to be careless and lose concentration. The reason for this is often quite simple and can be found in ill-fitting tack or even the wrong tack. Check the saddle fits your hose well and a good saddler will be only too pleased to help you. Check if there is any movement of the saddle when the horse is jumping. Check the girth is not pinching your horse when he is moving. We use thin show-girths most of the time because I find these give the horse's 'working parts', so to speak, more freedom to operate efficiently. Make a very careful check of the bridle, see if it fits properly and is not pinching somewhere such as round the ears and, particularly, the mouthpiece. See that it is the right size for your horse, especially around the lips.

That brings us to the very delicate and complicated question of what type of bit to use. We did touch on this very slightly earlier but it is a very difficult subject to advise on without seeing the horse and rider. I use mainly plain snaffle bits with a dropped noseband

and I very rarely use a martingale. If you are fortunate enough to buy your horse young and are able to develop him yourself then mouth problems will not develop. But often a small problem in jumping and riding can be overcome by changing the bit. I think international jumping rider, Harvey Smith, an expert on bits and bitting, sums it all up when he says:

> There's a bit for every horse somewhere. What suits one doesn't suit another. Some bits and combinations of bits may look harsh, but some horses relax in them . . . Any real horseman knows that the moment you abuse a horse in the mouth you can put him away in the field. Because if you have no mouth then you have no horse.

Incorrect Presentation by the Rider

This is, perhaps, the most common cause for careless jumping in the show ring. A rider should be able to feel that his horse is not meeting his fences right, if he can't then he is not ready to compete seriously. The trainer should also be able to see that horse and rider are not getting their presentation right or that the rider is not attacking his fences with a positive technique. This problem can be solved by putting in much more homework on presentation until it is right but if the rider continues to be weak in this area then his coach must take him back to the grids for more rhythm work until he really understands the importance of the jumping technique in terms of strides. Fred Broome Senior sums up this problem . . .

> Presentation has got to be absolutely 100 per cent correct, or perhaps it is fairer to say 98 per cent correct, otherwise you unbalance your horse . . . and that can cost you a rail! It's as simple as that really.

So carefully study what you are doing and how you are doing it. Over-riding a horse at a fence can cause just as many problems as under-riding. The art of a good effective jumping technique is a balance between the two.

Lack of Training

This can be overcome by returning to schooling on the flat. The horse should not be put into a serious jumping programme until he is going correctly, and working willingly to the rider's aids, on the flat. Equally, the rider should not start jumping training until he has an independent seat and is fully conversant with the techniques of riding on the flat. All this may seem obvious to many of you but many riders and trainers do ignore these vital points.

Faulty Training

Bad memories of another rider or trainer, or a bad fall, will result in a loss of confidence for the horse. Patience, understanding and long, quiet hours of work are the only solution to these problems.

Lack of Condition or Poor Health

A cause often overlooked because a horse can sometimes look healthy yet have something bothering him. So check him over for any soreness, especially of the shins, for lameness, for a sore back or a pulled muscle, for ill-fitting shoes and so on. Get his teeth checked regularly. If there are obvious signs of lack of condition or sudden weight-loss then rest the horse and consult your veterinary surgeon.

CHAPTER 8

Preparing for the Show

CLEAR ROUND JUMPING

Many Riding Club, Pony Club and local shows include what is called 'clear round jumping' in their schedule. These classes are a wonderful medium for introducing a novice horse to competition. The course is quite simple and often set at various levels throughout the day, evening or duration of the show. For example, in the mornings it will start off very low for ponies and young horses and later it is raised for those competitors who wish to have a serious school. The normal entry can be from as little as 50p to £2 depending on the standard of the show and if your horse jumps a clear round you collect a rosette.

The fences are proper show fences and these classes are very useful as a dress rehearsal before attempting a competitive class. All your work at home can be brought together without any pressure and your horse will get a quiet introduction to the atmosphere of a show. You can go in the clear round jumping as many times as you like so there is every opportunity to solve problems like over-excitement and stage-fright . . . and not just for your horse! With novice horses, and riders, I have always used these clear round classes, first, as a dummy run and second, as a warm-up before putting the horse into his main class of the day.

For your first show it is best to pick a local unaffiliated show or a schooling show. Unaffiliated shows are events which are not official British Show Jumping Association shows although they are all run to the same rules as the affiliated shows and the judges are often members of the BSJA's judges panel. The big difference between the two is that unaffiliated shows are restricted to the amount of prize money they can offer to competitors so the level of competition is kept to a standard which is ideally suited to novice horses and ponies.

The average schedule contains local novice jumping classes, for riders who live within a certain radius of the show, several novice's classes graded by the sizes of horses and ponies, ie 14.2hh and 15hh and over, speed classes, a small open class and a main open class. Within these schedules most show centres run their championship series on a points basis through the winter and summer seasons. These unaffiliated shows, properly run, are a first-class nursery for future showjumpers and riders as the conditions and atmosphere are very close to affiliated shows but with a more relaxed competitive attitude. Much will depend on what your own ambitions are but many riders find the unaffiliated circuit is as far as they want to go – or have the time for – and quite a few of them become local stars.

In America the equivalent would be schooling shows which are run during the winter and spring months and in Britain we are seeing more and more of this type of show being run by local centres. At schooling shows a well-known course designer is brought in to build courses suitable for horses from novice to open level which are being prepared for affiliated jumping.

NOVICE CLASSES

After you have had a satisfactory 'dummy run' over clear round courses you can take your horse back the following week to compete in one of the novice's classes.

The Jump-off

If all goes well you will most probably jump a clear round and qualify for a jump-off. This may not happen the first time you compete in a real class, of course, but it will eventually. Don't suddenly ask your horse to go against the clock. After all the slow, careful and patient work you put in schooling your horse to go smoothly, calmly and correctly, a sudden demand for speed-jumping will destroy that solid and well-laid foundation. It is far better, and wiser, to ride him for just another smooth clear round. Do this for three or four jump-offs asking for just a little bit more speed on each outing. Galloping is not showjumping . . . if you fall into that trap all you will be doing is encouraging your horse to start flattening over his fences and you will start getting him over-excited each time he enters the arena.

Once again it is a case of make haste slowly. The winning rosettes will come all in good time. The early days of competing are the same as the early stages of jumping training. Each step must be planned and regulated . . . rather like building a house, brick by brick. Your 'feel' becomes the judge of the rate of progress. As you, the rider, feel your horse gain in confidence and accuracy so you can start looking for areas, like turns or turn-backs, in the jump-off course where you feel you can take a shorter route. The art of winning jump-offs is to find a shorter route than your rivals rather than setting off like a steeplechaser trying to win a race.

If the course designer has set a turn through 45° from a line of three fences to a line of two fences on a diagonal down the centre of the arena. As you feel your horse gaining confidence in the ring, jumping carefully, fluently and concentrating on what he is doing, you can start asking a few questions on that turn. As you land from the third fence on the first line let your horse take at least three non-jumping strides before asking him to make the turn towards the two centre fences. The next time you can cut that to two non-jumping strides and eventually to one non-jumping stride. All those hours spent schooling your horse to go away from you and to come back to you the instant you ask is now going to pay off and when it does it is not only a great sight to see but also a wonderful feeling of satisfaction particularly when you know you have not scrambled your horse's mind to achieve it!

Jump-offs, at national level, go in a drawn order made after the preliminary rounds. So if you find yourself drawn first to go, study the jump-off course plan, which will be on the board in the collecting ring, and see if you can see a short route. But, above all, when you get in the arena ride for a clear round. You are always in with a chance if you have a clear round on your score-card. If you are drawn in the middle or at the end of the finalists then take advantage of the time you have available to watch the others go and, once more, look for the turns you think you can make shorter than your competitors. (In international jumping the jump-off order is the same as the original starting drawn order in the preliminary round.)

When you reach the stage where you are jumping clear rounds regularly each weekend then you can start thinking about moving up a gear to affiliated shows.

AFFILIATED SHOWS

In order to compete at affiliated shows you must become a member of the British Show Jumping Association and register your horse with the association. From the first time he competes (affiliated) your horse's winnings will be recorded by the association. All novices start in the bottom grade, Grade C.

The BSJA runs several series of novice classes such as Path-finders, Discovery Stakes etc. You and your horse's progress will now be controlled by your performance. The more prize money you win the higher up the grades you will go. If you and your horse are good enough you may make it to the top grade, Grade A, and be talent-spotted and invited to compete internationally. There have been rare occasions when this has happened but normally to succeed to international level a rider needs to be showjumping full time and have at least three Grade A horses.

For most owner/riders Grade A is not the object of the exercise mainly because it is time-consuming and also because it is very costly unless you can be certain of winning prize money consistently. That does not mean that the owner/rider cannot be ambitious about his or her showjumping. Riding clubs hold their own competitions including regional and national series leading to a championship. It is through these that the real amateur rider can get a chance of qualifying for a major show and to ride internationally in a riding club team. If you have not got a riding club in your area then get some friends together and form one. The British Horse Society will be delighted to help you establish it and your local equestrian centre will be only too pleased to provide the facilities.

PREPARING FOR THE SHOW

Clean all your tack, riding gear and the horse's clothing the night before. Check that you have plenty of spares like stirrup leathers, reins, girths, jumping studs etc – all the items that may break or get lost.

Go to the stables early that morning, muck out your horse's box and give him a light feed. While your horse is enjoying his breakfast you and your helpers – usually the family – can be loading up all the tack and gear into the motor horsebox or trailer. Two travelling containers will be needed for the equipment, one for your horse and the other for spare items of equipment. Put in two full haynets, enough feed for the day, water buckets, water containers and a medicine basket or box with first-aid kit for both equines and humans. Your own veterinary surgeon will advise on the items you will need in the first-aid box. Take a large torch, grooming equipment, spare plaiting-up material and waterproof clothing for you and your horse.

When all that is done check that your horse has eaten his feed, put the headcollar on him and tie him up. Remove the night rugs but if you like to see a nice plaited mane for showing, now is the time to do it. Plaiting manes is, perhaps, a little old fashioned now in jumping but I still like to see it and it certainly keeps the mane out of the hands of the rider!

Plaiting

Six plaits are the norm including the forelock but the number of plaits you put in will depend on the length of your horse's neck and/or the thickness of his mane. Materials required are: a water brush; a mane comb; a reel of strong thread (the same colour as the mane ie brown, black or white); a needle with a large eye and a pair of scissors. First cut some lengths of thread about 8in (15cm) long and lay them out on a clean stable rubber so that you can see them clearly. Then, wet the mane down with the water brush. Divide the mane with the mane comb into five equal parts. Start plaiting at the poll by dividing a portion of mane into three equal strands. When you get about two-thirds of the way down, take one of the lengths of thread by its middle and start plaiting it in. On reaching the end of the plait, take the two ends of the thread and pass them around the end of the plait and pull tight. When all the plaits are done just stand back to see that they are all about the same thickness. Then take the needle and pass the two ends of the thread through the eye, double the plait under itself and pass the needle through the plait. Pull the ends of the thread through the needle, put the needle away (in your lapel or sweater) take the two ends again, bind the thread around the plait and then knot it at the top of the plait. Cut any excess pieces of thread away with the scissors. The finished product should look pleasing to the eye with even and tight plaits close to the horse's crest.

There are other methods, like using elastic bands, but these do not give such a pleasing result as the needle and thread.

The next job is to put on the tail bandage. First dampen and straighten the top hairs of the tail with the water brush. Then take a bandage and unroll about 8in (15cm) of it, place your left hand under the tail, holding the unrolled portion of the bandage while your right hand holds the roll. Pass the unrolled bandage under the tail with your left hand and set it at a slight upward angle. Now start turning the roll around the tail with your right hand. Make one complete turn and then turn over the corner of the first portion that was placed into position by your left hand. Continue down the tail in uniform turns and keep a fairly tight pressure on the bandage. On reaching the end, secure the bandage by the tapes and roll in the loose ends. Lift the tail away from the hocks and bend it into a comfortable and straight form. When you arrive at the showground you can remove the tail bandage by simply grasping it at the nearest point to the horse's dock and pull it down.

The next task is to 'quarter' the horse by giving him a light brushing. Remove any overnight stains and sponge out his eyes, nostrils and dock. Then pick his feet out and grease them with hoof oil. Put on his travelling rug, with a blanket underneath if it is a very cold morning. At this stage the travelling boots or bandages can be put on all four legs. Load your horse into the trailer and allow plenty of time to reach the showground. Now it is all systems go for the first serious show.

WARMING UP

On arrival check the time of your class again, unload your horse and prepare to warm up. It is very difficult to advise, and risky to generalise, about warming up at a show. Horses, like human athletes, differ enormously in the amount of warming up they need. An example of this was two super ponies my eldest daughter used to showjump when she was small. The Welsh-bred William, for instance, needed very little warming up but he had to be kept on the move just before his turn to go into the arena. Then he would canter straight in with his eyes sparkling, ears cocked, with that 'getting down to business' look about him. Whereas Fiddler, who was also Welsh bred, needed a lot of time with plenty of flat-work, half-halting, changes of rein, circles, small and large, and several practice jumps at the trot and canter. Then he had to be allowed to think it was all over for about ten minutes before he went in. Then he was ready for action. So there is no way anyone can give hard-and-fast rules on warming up.

Two tips I can give you are: warm up well on the flat and over small fences; then warm up over a spread first followed by a vertical but do not fall into the trap of jumping your horse too high or too wide in the practice ring – the arena is the place for that. It is better to under-do your warming up rather than overdo it. You will

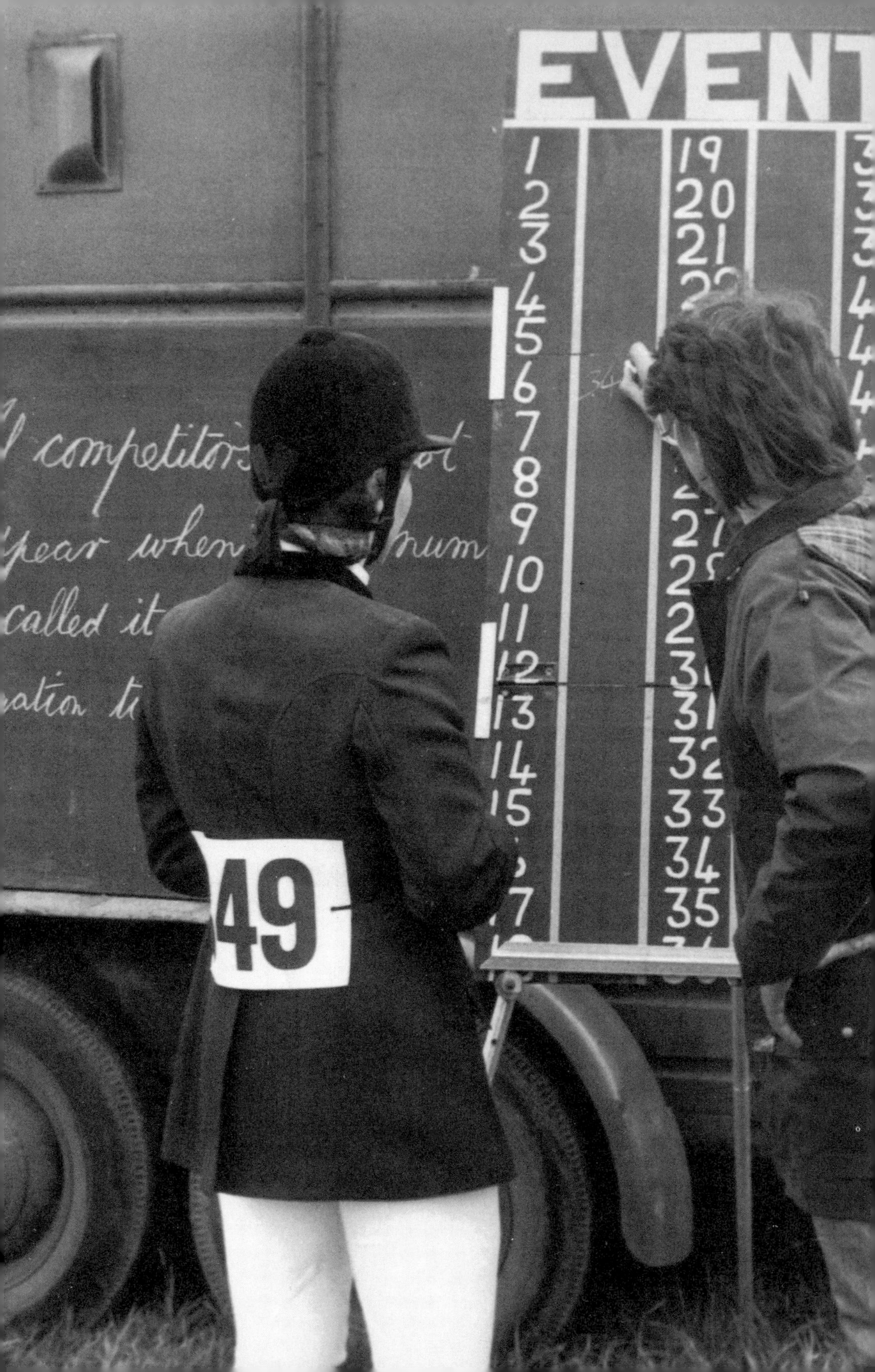
EVENT
competitors
pear when
num
called it
ation
49

Before you start warming-up for your class, get
your number down on the start board. If it's your
horse's first show then put in at about the halfway
stage on the list. This will give you time to watch a
few competitors go so that you study how the course
is riding. Once the class has started, get
somebody to check on how many there are to go
before your turn. Above all, be ready to go when the
collecting ring steward calls you up

Always have somebody on the ground helping you to warm up, not only for safety or for putting rails up, but also to help you and your horse get ready for competition. A knowledgeable helper can often see more easily how your horse is going than you can from the saddle

Take a bit of a break after warming up and just let your horse have a look at everything around him and, if possible, everything around the show ring

soon, by experience, be able to judge what is just right for your horse. I have seen too many contests lost in the practice ring and not enough won there so use your intelligence and experience. Don't be tempted to impress in the practice ring.

WALKING THE COURSE

This is where things really do begin to get serious. Never under-estimate the value of walking the course and certainly never rush it. Allow yourself plenty of time first to study the course plan and take in the jump-off course as well. As you walk into the arena stop for a few minutes and study the general layout. Get the relationship between the entry to the arena and the first fence firmly fixed in your mind. Then plan where you are going to circle while waiting for the starting bell or klaxon.

Often you see riders huddled around talking, or just wandering from one fence to another, but this is not the way to walk the course and certainly not the way to win competitions. It is far better to set off with your coach, or one of your parents, and start at the very beginning – the approach to the start line. Set out to walk the com-plete track you will be taking with your horse, working out the turns, how you are going to use the space available in the arena and the state of the ground. Is it uphill or downhill in places? Where are the rough patches in the footing? Where are the smooth patches? Inspect each fence individually, touch them, feel them, try to get to know each one and its characteristics. Where fences are set close together stride out the distance. You know your horse's stride so work out how many strides you think you will need to present him at a fence well.

In double and treble combinations try to measure the inside dis-tances by striding them from an imaginary line which you think will be the highest point of your horse's jump to his highest point over the second or third elements. With this information you can decide whether the double and treble are going to ride long or short. Finally stand in the middle of the arena and talk yourself through the course: 'There's the first fence, then come on the right rein to the second, then back to the third,' and so on.

(pp 168-9)
When walking the course, have a good look at all the fences and walk the track you intend taking with your horse, especially any turns or changes of rein

RIDING THE COURSE

If you are not among the first to go, watch the other competitors jump so that you can judge how the course is riding. Then when it comes to your turn, get into the ring quickly, keep your horse on the move and canter him around the fences so that he can get some idea of where he is but don't, of course, actually 'show' him any particular fence because you may risk elimination by the judges.

Always approach the first fence on a straight line, through the middle of the starting 'gate', and go for the middle of the fence. How you jump the first fence will tell you how you are going to jump the rest of the course. But, let's assume, you have a rail off the first fence which can often happen for the beginner through nerves or lack of concentration and after that things get worse the further they go around the course. If this does happen then switch your mind to imagine that the second fence is the first fence. Simple but it often works.

Throughout the course take a line which will give you a straight approach to each fence and always ride for the centre of each obstacle. When the turns come make them long and sweeping so that your horse has plenty of time to settle and concentrate on where he is going. The easiest trap a novice rider falls into when he is first competing in the ring is to rush things. They try to get to each fence too quickly. They try too hard and get over-keen to show what they can do. This is where starting at unaffiliated level is such good value. All those nerves and tensions are soon ironed out with absolutely no pressures.

Take it slow and steady . . . enjoy yourself in the ring and you will find that your horse will too. Above all, don't be tempted to rush the last couple of fences. Ride them as you did the first part of the course and then, after landing from the last, let your horse just canter on through the finishing line and literally pull himself up. Don't whatever you do pull your horse up sharply immediately after going through the finish line. Why one sees so many riders do this I really do not know. There is absolutely no gain in it, in fact, quite the opposite. It unsettles a horse and it puts physical strain on his back and joints. Just let your horse see it is all over by dropping your hands after clearing the finish line, rub your horse's neck and talk to him. He will realise it is all over and will gradually pull himself up. Then let him walk out of the arena relaxed and on a loose rein.

Stride out the distances between the elements of a double or treble combination and decide whether you see them as long or short non-jumping strides for your horse

Once back in the collecting ring loosen off your girth and dismount. Loosen the dropped noseband, run the irons up the leathers but make a fuss of your horse too. Let him see that you have both worked hard at home, you have come to the show, gone into the arena and everything has come together. Horses do seem to be able to understand this. Then place a summer sheet, paddock sheet or blanket, over him depending on what time of year it is and take him for a quiet walk around. Even if you have qualified for a jump-off let your horse relax for a few minutes.

When it is all over take off all his tack and again cover him up. Then let him have a drink and a short feed or a bit of grass before getting ready to load up and head for home.

BACK HOME

Try to arrange, well in advance, for somebody to prepare the loose box during the time the horse has been away so that he comes home to a warm box and clean fresh bedding and water. Once your horse has settled back into his box take off his tail bandage and travelling gear. Then leave him alone for some thirty minutes to unwind and most probably have a lovely roll.

Come back to let his plaits down, brush him over and rug him up for the night. Put up a sweet-smelling hay net and feed a gruel or bran mash, and turn him loose for the night. Later that night it is worth just going down to the yard to see that your horse has settled down and eaten all his feed. Check the water bucket, shake up the bedding and have a quiet look round to see if there are any knocks or swellings after the day's competitions. Finally check all bolts and ventilation and leave him to enjoy a good night's rest.

Then it is back to the house to relive the day and have the inevitable post-mortem on performance come win or lose!

International course designer, Alan Oliver, measures the distance of the preliminary round and the jump-off course, and from this the time allowed for both trips is calculated. This same system is used at all shows affiliated to the British Show Jumping Association

CHAPTER 9

Care of Equipment

The equine athlete, like any other sporting performer, must have efficient equipment which is well looked after. Many a good class has been lost through the breakage of stirrup leathers and reins but the chances of this happening can be kept to a minimum by regularly cleaning and checking all equipment. So let us go through the organisation and care required to look after your equipment so that it will last and, above all, be safe to use.

STORAGE

A workshop, garage, or garden shed will serve very well as a tack-room and equipment store. Bridles should be kept on a round or half-moon shaped holder so that they do not lose their shape. The best form of saddle-rack is either a steel 'saddle-shaped' frame of about 18in (45cm) in length, or a wooden frame, in a reversed 'V'-shape, attached either to the saddle-room wall or to a free-standing wooden saddle-horse.

The stirrup leathers, irons and girths should be taken off the saddle and hung on individual hooks. This ensures that the leathers and girths are kept flat. All martingales, if you use them, should be hung by the neck-strap. A stable rubber makes an effective dust cover for saddles but if you can get saddle-covers so much the better.

The tack-room should be dry, with an even temperature, although leather tack should not be kept close to artificial heating. Rugs, blankets, boots, exercise sheets etc can be stored in a box or trunk while leg bandages, tail bandages and so on can be kept in a drawer or cupboard. All these items of horse clothing must be dry and clean before being put away or stored. If it is necessary to store tack for long periods, cover all the leather parts with a thin coating of Vaseline or neatsfoot oil. This treatment will protect the leather and keep it in good condition.

CLEANING

Materials needed for cleaning tack are:

- Some form of protective overall or apron.
- A tin of saddle soap, or a bar of glycerine saddle soap.
- A softening agent, eg vegetable oil.
- Metal polish.
- Two sponges – one for applying saddle soap and one for cleaning.
- A duster or soft cloth for polishing.
- Two stable rubbers – one for drying, the other to act as a dust cover.
- A burnisher for irons and bits made of plain steel and some silver sand. (These are items rarely used now due to the wide use of nickel plate.)
- A chamois leather for drying.
- A dandy brush for brushing dirt from serge linings.
- A narrow piece of wood, or something similar, for cleaning out awkward areas such as leather holes, buckles etc.
- A rubber or plastic bucket three-quarters full with luke-warm water and no artificial cleaning agent added.

The Saddle

First strip the saddle of leathers, irons, girth buckle guards, girth and numnah, if one is used. Place the saddle on the saddle-horse. Take the irons off the leathers and place them in the bucket. Put the leathers and girth over the saddle-horse. Tack-cleaning time is a perfect opportunity for inspecting equipment for any signs of wear and tear, or faults. Pay particular attention to checking all stitching, buckles and girth straps. We start with the saddle as this can then be left to dry while the other items are cleaned. Most modern jumping saddles are now leather lined so this can be sponged clean with a damp sponge, wiping all the sweat and dirt deposits away. Now the entire saddle can be sponged over and then dried with the chamois leather. The chamois should be soaked in water and then wrung out before use.

The saddle is now ready for soaping. Take a damp sponge and cover it fairly generously with saddle soap. Then start with the underside, applying the soap in circular movements, but remember that tack-cleaning is not just a tidying-up process, it is also a way of feeding the leather, so work the soap in well. Place the saddle on the saddle-horse, repeat the process on the seat, skirt, panels, flaps and girth tabs, giving the underside of the leather, especially the flaps, a thorough coating. The underside is more absorbent, being the flesh side of the hide, so plenty of soap will be required on the sponge. Then treat the saddle with neatsfoot oil or vegetable oil, these feed the leather and keep it soft. If any leather is to be stored for a long time a generous coating of either product will keep it in tip-top condition. The oil is better applied with the hands because you can then work it well into the leather. When all is done, place the saddle on the saddle-rack and cover with a stable rubber or a dust-cover.

Numnahs
Numnahs are made of sheepskin or felt so brush well or wash. Make sure they are well dried and aired before use.

Girths
Attention must be given to the condition of the girth when cleaning no matter what material it is made from. The girth is the rider's lifeline so any defects such as fraying, broken strands on string or nylon girths, splits or cracks on webbing or leather girths, must be attended to immediately. The best treatment for a worn or damaged girth is to throw it away!

The stitching at the buckles is another danger point but this can often be repaired by a saddler. A girth in poor condition, or one that has been neglected, can seriously injure both horse and rider. Girth galls, sore elbows or sore ribs will be the result for your horse and these ailments will not clear up quickly when your horse is in serious training. So don't take any chances with poor standard girths.

LEATHER GIRTHS
Clean with soap in the same way as the saddle and clean the buckles. For the folded type of leather girth it is worth treating the inside with neatsfoot oil to keep the leather soft. After cleaning hang up all girths by the buckles to keep them in good shape.

WEB, STRING AND NYLON GIRTHS
These should be well brushed daily but they do have a tendency to

go hard so washing with pure soap (flakes or liquid) will be necessary at least once a week. They must be completely dry before re-use. Be careful with some string or nylon girths as these can shrink. Coloured girths will, in some cases, lose a certain amount of their colour when washed.

STIRRUP LEATHERS

Wash carefully and then saddle soap. At the same time check that the stitching is in good order and examine carefully for signs of wear and tear in the leather. Many a good showjumping class has been lost by a broken stirrup leather! Clean the buckles and finally see that all the holes are free of soap, oil or dirt deposits. (Use the narrow piece of wood in your tack-cleaning kit.) Hang up the stirrup leather by the buckles to store.

STIRRUP IRONS

Wash in the bucket of water and then dry with a stable rubber or a soft cloth. See that the 'eye' of the iron is clean and that it is not mis-shapen or has worn thin. Too much play between the leather and the area of the 'eye' can be dangerous. Rubber treads that fit into the base of the irons have become essential in any jumping rider's tackroom. Their aim is to help you keep the ball of your foot on the iron, leaving your heels and ankles free to give support and balance to your seat. These rubber treads should removed from the irons and washed regularly.

THE BRIDLE

About once a month bridles should be taken apart completely and each part thoroughly sponged clean before being given a generous coating of neatsfoot oil or saddle soap. And once more this is a good time to check on the condition of the bridle and the bit.

For daily cleaning, though, it is not necessary to take the bridle completely apart. Just take the noseband off, if you use one, drop the cheekpieces down to the last hole and place the mouthpiece only in the bucket of luke-warm water and wash. Next wipe the headpiece clean with a damp sponge and hang the bridle on a hook or over the saddle-horse. Now with the damp sponge wipe the rest of the bridle clean. The sponge can be curled over so that both sides of the leather are cleaned at the same time. Sponge the reins, start at the union with the mouthpiece and pull the sponge all the way down to the buckle. Reins vary considerably today according to

179

personal tastes; plain leather; plaited leather; nylon and rubber covered, so your cleaning technique will depend on the type you have and which material they are made from. Next sponge the browband and then the dropped noseband. The complete bridle can now be dried with the chamois leather and the saddle soap applied, treating both the inside and the outside of the leather. Dry and polish the mouthpiece with a soft cloth, or a stable rubber, but don't use metal polish. With the narrow piece of wood, clear all dirt deposits from the moving parts of the bit and free the holes and keepers of the bridle from soap or water deposits. Finally adjust all the buckles back to their normal positions and hang the bridle up on a bridle rack.

Horse Clothing

All rugs, night and day versions, paddock sheets, exercise quarter sheets etc must be cleaned regularly. From time to time they should be well washed and scrubbed or, if possible, dry-cleaned. Summer sheets and rugs, for example, can be cleaned around the end of October before being stored for the winter months and winter clothing should be dry-cleaned or washed around mid-April before being stored for the summer months. Preventative measures, though, will be needed to guard against damage from moths and damp during storage.

Other Items

Modern materials now used for the making and design of jumping boots and over-reach boots have simplified cleaning and care techniques to a basic minimum of just washing and/or brushing.

Jumping Studs

Anti-slip heel studs (jumping studs) are fitted to the shoes of jumping horses especially when they have to perform on poor or wet surfaces. But even in summertime a good dry grass surface can become greasy. It is necessary, therefore, to have shoes fitted that are specially designed to take the studs. These shoes have a threaded hole at each heel, either one or two to each foot depending on which type of stud is used. Your farrier will be pleased to advise on the merits of various studs. The studs are fitted by screwing them into these ready-made holes but when the studs are not in use the holes should be packed with cotton wool to protect the thread and to keep any dirt particles or mud from blocking them up.

Care of Practice Fences and Schooling Area

This is one area of maintenance which is often neglected but nonetheless is an essential part of efficiency in any modern show-jumping yard. Keep your jumping rails, fillers and wings bright and clean. If the paintwork gets chipped or peeled take a day off from intense schooling and enjoy yourself with some brushes and pots of paint. Check for any cracks or splits in the jumping rails. If you catch this type of wear and tear early the rails can be banded but if the damage has weakened the rail or put it out of shape it's wiser to replace it. The schooling area, whether it be wood-bark, sand, or grass, will need daily raking. With a grass or sand surface, a run over with a chain harrow or a ridged roller about twice a week will keep the footing in good condition.

Conclusion: The Future

We started off at the beginning of this book discussing attitude, aptitude and the relationship between horse and rider. All these aspects are shared by everyone involved in horse sports to some degree or another. But the marvellous thing about showjumping is that you do not have to be a potential Olympian to enjoy it. There is something for everybody. The sport has seen some vital changes over the past few years. Most people coming into the sport now do not come from the traditional horse- or farming-culture backgrounds. In fact, several leading riders gained their first experience in the saddle at a local riding school.

Through the British Horse Society's instructor qualification system, teaching has become more standardised which has produced young riders who may not have the natural instinctive gifts of a David Broome or a Harvey Smith but who ride in a technically correct way and get good results. The 1976 Olympic individual gold medallist, Alwin Schockemöhle, once said:

> If there is a secret to the game, it's getting the right instructor at the very beginning of your career, and as for the horse it's the level of the handling he has experienced *before* he starts jumping training that counts.

He was making two very important points. Firstly, getting the right instructor means not necessarily the most celebrated, but the right one for you. This is the instructor whom you like, you feel you can work with and you feel has the professional ability and experience to bring you through each phase of your riding career at just the right time.

Gerry Mullins on Glendalough competing at the 1988 Olympic Games in Seoul, South Korea. Course designer Olaf Petersen's fences at those games were an absolute work of art and has influenced the design of fences around the world ever since. Modern courses are not just a test of horses and riders they have now become a pleasure to look at for spectators

Secondly, the standard of the horse's training on the flat will determine not only how good a showjumper he is going to be but also how consistent a performer he will be in the show ring. But that schooling on the flat will only be as good as you are and can only be effective if carried out progressively and regularly.

There is one side of riding training which too many riders tend to overlook and that is their own fitness. No rider can do justice to a well-conditioned, well-schooled horse unless he himself is in good physical shape. Riding in itself is good exercise and running around looking after a horse will keep you in some sort of shape. But study your own diet and physical condition as much as you do that of your horse. Above all, don't attempt to ride a schooling session if you are feeling tired, have a cold or are worried about something. These things will affect the evenness of your temper and one bad schooling session can destroy the good work of previous months.

The influence of flat-work on the showjumper is becoming stronger with the passing of each season. No matter at what level you compete there will always be plenty of good riders and horses which can jump. The winning margin is often the best-schooled horse and the most accurate rider.

Courses, again at all levels, are getting more technical as the standard of riding and jumping improves. Designers bring in complications with short and long distances in treble combinations and with related distances on straight lines. Related distances exist when fences are set at five to six non-jumping strides apart and a designer can set an accuracy test of say a spread fence to a vertical. In other words he is sending horse and rider forward and then putting them back again. In doing so he is testing the ability of the competitors on the flat as well as by the dimensions of his fences.

We are, thankfully, seeing more and more of this type of emphasis replacing classes which develop into 'galloping' contests. Jumping and accuracy on the flat is once more the name of the game. Most horses and riders can be schooled to jump a 3ft (0.9m) class but if they are encouraged to gallop round such a course they find themselves scoring too many faults when the real showjumping starts over a 3ft 9in (1.15m) course.

Janet Hunter, again, with Lisnamarrow, this time competing at Douglas Bunn's All England Jumping Course, Hickstead, Sussex. Douglas's colourful fences and landscaped 'dressing' are as much part of the Hickstead sporting spectacle as the competitions

The swing towards correct riding and schooling has gained more momentum by the introduction of clear rounds counting more than fast times. In several of the novice series run by the BSJA, such as the Foxhunter, with regional finals leading to an annual final, horses can qualify through the number of clear rounds in the preliminary classes. This move has been greeted, by amateurs and professionals alike, as one of the most positive and progressive changes the sport has seen for some time. It encourages *clean* jumping as opposed to *sloppy* jumping. In doing so this trend has added the satisfaction of riding correctly to the fun of taking part in the sport.

Throughout the world, in Britain, Europe, North America and Australasia, we are seeing showjumping as a participation sport, grow each year. New equestrian centres are being opened with superb modern facilities, indoor and outdoor, for jumping shows at all levels. The domesticated horse has been with us for 2,000 years or more and as part of our leisure or sporting careers, he is certainly going to remain with us for a very, very long time to come.

Simplified Rules of Showjumping

Under British Show Jumping Association Rules:

- There are no marks or faults for style.
- Each fence is judged separately.
- Knocking down a fence – 4 faults.
- Refusals: first 3 faults; second 6 faults; third elimination. Refusals are cumulative and the third refusal in a complete round eliminates the competitor.
- Fall of horse or rider – 8 faults.
- Time: the course has to be completed within a time allowed which is based on the number of yards per minute required by the conditions of the competition. Exceeding the time allowed is penalised at the rate of a quarter of a fault for every second or part second over the time allowed. The time limit is double the time allowed. Exceeding the time limit results in elimination.
- Where there is a jump-off of competitors on equal scores, the rider with the fastest time and the least faults wins.
- In affiliated jumping all horses or ponies, riders and/or owners must be registered with or be members of the British Show Jumping Association.

Acknowledgements

My sincere thanks to Maureen Collins and her sponsor, Stewart Hamilton of ADS Office Telecommunications Limited, for letting us use their very understanding young horse, Roll On Fair Thrill, better known to his friends as Rollo.

Grateful thanks, too, to Philip and Jennifer Oldham, owners of the West End Equestrian Centre in Buckinghamshire, for kindly letting us use their facilities.

Also to my eldest daughter Adrienne, better known to her friends as Addie, for acting, as she has done in other books of mine, the role of pupil. I taught and trained Addy in her riding from a very early age, and working with her during the years when she was competing in pony jumping, working hunter pony and dressage was an absolute joy and privilege for me.

Finally my thanks to my colleague, photographer Bob Langrish. Bob never pretends to be an expert on horses or equitation, but with a camera he has a natural feeling for instructional photography.

Peter Churchill

Some Useful Addresses

The British Horse Society
British Equestrian Centre
Stoneleigh
Kenilworth
Warwickshire CV8 2LR Tel: 0203 696697

The British Show Jumping Association
British Equestrian Centre
Stoneleigh
Kenilworth
Warwickshire CV8 2LR Tel: 0203 696516

The Association of British Riding Schools
The Secretary
Old Brewery Yard
Penzance
Cornwall TR18 2SL

British Equestrian Trade Association
Wothersome Grange
Bramham
Nr Wetherby
Yorkshire LS23 6YL Tel. 0532 892267

British Equine Veterinary Association
Admin Secretary
Park Lodge
Bells Yew Green Road
Frant
Tunbridge Wells
Kent TN3 9EB Tel: 089 275 368

British Veterinary Association
Mr James Baird
Chief Executive
7 Mansfield Street
Portland Place
London W1M 0AT Tel: 01 636 6541

Federation Equestre Internationale (FEI)
Schosshaldenstrasse 32
CH – 3000
Berne 32
Switzerland

Index

David & Charles' Equestrian Titles

Behaviour Problems in Horses · Susan McBane
Breeding and Training a Horse or Pony · Ann Sutcliffe
Champion Horses and Ponies · Pamela Macgregor-Morris
Clarissa Strachan's Young Event Horse · Clarissa Strachan
Complete Horse · Johannes E. Flade
Dressage Begin the Right Way · Lockie Richards
Effective Horse and Pony Management · Susan McBane
Equine Fitness · Dr David Snow and Colin Vogel
Going the Distance A Manual of Long-Distance Riding · Sue
  Parslow
Gymkhana! · Lesley Eccles and Linda Burgess
The Heavy Horse Manual · Nick Rayner and Keith Chivers
The Horse and the Law · Donald Cassell
Horse Breeding · Peter Rossdale
Horse Driving Trials The Art of Competitive Coachmanship ·
  Tom Coombs
**The Horse's Health from A to Z – An Equine Veterinary
  Dictionary (new edition)** · Peter Rossdale and Susan M. Wreford
The Horse Owner's Handbook · Monty Mortimer
The Horse Rider's Handbook · Monty Mortimer
Hunting An Introductory Handbook · R. W. F. Poole
The Imperial Horse The Saga of the Lipizzaners · Hans-Heinrich
  Isenbart and Emil Buhrer
Keeping a Horse Outdoors · Susan McBane
Lungeing The Horse and Rider · Sheila Inderwick
A Passion for Ponies · John and Francesca Bullock
Practical Dressage · Jane Kidd
Practical Showing · Nigel Hollings
The Riding Instructor's Handbook · Monty Mortimer
Riding and Stable Safety · Ann Brock
The Stable Veterinary Handbook · Colin J. Vogel
Transporting Your Horse or Pony · Chris Larter and Tony Jackson
Understanding Horses · Garda Langley

PRACTICAL SHOWING · Nigel Hollings

Nigel Hollings firmly believes that you never stop learning when producing horses and ponies for the show ring. During a career which began in childhood and spans over twenty years, he has collected a wealth of practical experience in the modern world of showing, and in this book he draws together the strands of that experience for the benefit of all those with an interest in the sport.

In his highly readable and original style, and with the help of many excellent photographs, Nigel Hollings guides the reader through the search for that elusive champion, and explains in detail how to school and prepare him or her for the show ring. It is this attention to the smallest detail, in everything from stable management to sewing in the last plait, that the author suggests is the key to success. Freely giving away his 'tricks of the trade' he discusses tack and turnout, and how to create the right 'picture' through a combination of ringcraft, showmanship and an understanding of what the judge will be looking for in the different classes.

Like judging, the production of horses and ponies for the show ring is very much a matter of personal opinion, and it is on this basis that Nigel Hollings has produced this down-to-earth guide to showing. An essentially practical book which will prove an invaluable source of reference for both the novice and more experienced exhibitor, it is nevertheless stamped with a sense of humour – without which, the author suggests, you will not survive for long in the showing game!

The Author

Nigel Hollings started riding at the age of seven, and within five years had made history by becoming the first (and to date the only) boy to win the coveted Show Pony of the Year award at Wembley, riding Snailwell Charles. For two whole seasons he and Downland Smuggler dominated the working hunter pony classes, and Nigel then moved on to become a regular competitor on the northern point-to-point circuit, which helped him to make a very successful transition from ponies to horses.

In 1978 Nigel opened his own showing yard in partnership with his brother Stuart, and from here he has ridden and produced numerous champions, from Arab stallions to heavyweight hunters – exactly ten years after his own success as a rider, he produced the Show Pony of the Year at Wembley.

Nigel Hollings is a member of six different showing societies' judging panels – in several cases the youngest ever to be appointed – and is a Council member of the British Show Pony Society. He lives in Clayton-le-Dale, Lancashire.

PRACTICAL DRESSAGE · Jane Kidd

Dressage is the fastest growing of all equestrian sports in Britain and the USA, and yet it remains shrouded in mystery. In this book Jane Kidd, a leading dressage writer and internationally successful competitor, has peeled away the layers of this mystery to present this fascinating discipline in a way that is at once clear, straightforward and practical.

The book treats dressage as the control and development of the horse's natural athleticism. The author begins by analysing the special talents needed by a dressage horse, and explains a number of techniques for maximising natural ability, both human and equine. She then moves on to examine the all-important – and often neglected – basic principles of dressage. With the help of over one hundred photographs, many in helpful sequences, plus detailed explanatory captions, the reader is guided through the various movements required in dressage tests up to advanced level, the training of the horse to fulfil these requirements, and finally the preparation for and riding of the test on the day.

This clearly written, well illustrated and entirely practical book will appeal to all those with an interest in dressage, and will enable riders, judges and spectators alike to appreciate and enjoy their sport to the full.

The Author

Jane Kidd has ridden internationally in both show jumping and dressage, and is an official dressage judge and past member of the Dressage Committee. She is the official dressage correspondent for *Horse and Hound*, and reports shows for this magazine. She is the author of numerous books including *Festival of Dressage*, and is the British Horse Society's Training and Examinations Committee book compiler. Jane lives in Ewhurst, Surrey.

In preparation:
PRACTICAL EVENTING · Jane Holderness-Roddam
PRACTICAL HORSEMASTERSHIP · Susan McBane